THE Power OF A Positive Woman

[handwritten inscription]
Minden ellyizete, Congratulation
on your achievement
Peter-Cliff

About the Author

Karol Ladd is making a positive impact in the lives of today's purpose-filled women. She is a graduate of Baylor University and the author of twelve books including her bestseller *The Power of a Positive Mom*. Formerly a teacher, Karol now applies her leadership skills to deliver a message of hope to women in all walks of life. Her vivacious personality makes her a popular speaker to numerous women's groups and organizations each year. She serves on several boards and is president of Positive Life Principles, Inc. Karol lives in Dallas, Texas, with husband, Curt, and daughters, Grace and Joy. You can visit Karol at her Web site: Positvelifeprinciples.com

The Power of a Positive Woman

Karol Ladd

HOWARD
PUBLISHING CO.

Our purpose at Howard Publishing is to:
- *Increase faith* in the hearts of growing Christians
- *Inspire holiness* in the lives of believers
- *Instill hope* in the hearts of struggling people everywhere

Because He's coming again!

The Power of a Positive Woman © 2002 by Karol Ladd
All rights reserved. Printed in the United States of America

Published by Howard Publishing Co., Inc.,
3117 North 7th Street, West Monroe, Louisiana 71291-2227

02 03 04 05 06 07 08 09 10 11   10 9 8 7 6 5 4 3 2 1

Edited by Michele Buckingham
Interior design by Stephanie Denney and John Luke
Cover design by LinDee Loveland

Library of Congress Cataloging-in-Publication Data

Ladd, Karol.
  The power of a positive woman / Karol Ladd.
    p. cm.
  Includes bibliographical references
  ISBN 1-58229-267-1
    1. Women--Religious life. I. Title.

BV4527 .L252 2002
248.8'43--dc21

2002027476

Scripture quotations not otherwise marked are from the Holy Bible, New International
Version. Copyright © 1973, 1978, 1984 International Bible Society. Used by permission of
Zondervan Bible Publishers. All rights reserved. Scripture quotations marked NKJV are
taken from the New King James Version. Copyright © 1979, 1980, 1982 by Thomas
Nelson, Inc. Used by permission. All rights reserved. Scripture quotations marked NLT are
taken from the Holy Bible, New Living Translation, copyright © 1996. Used by permis-
sion of Tyndale House Publishers, Inc., Wheaton, Illinois 60189. All rights reserved.
Scriptures marked NASB are taken from the NEW AMERICAN STANDARD BIBLE ®,
copyright 1960, 1962, 1963, 1968, 1971, 1972, 1973, 1975, 1977, 1995 by The
Lockman Foundation. Used by permission. Scripture quotations marked KJV are from the
Holy Bible, Authorized King James Version. Public domain. Verses marked TLB are taken
from *The Living Bible,* copyright © 1971. Used by permission of Tyndale House
Publishers, Inc., Wheaton, Illinois 60189. All rights reserved.

Contents

Contents

Power Principle #4: Becoming a Woman of Joy

Power Principle #5: Becoming a Woman of Love

Power Principle #6: Becoming a Woman of Courage

Power Principle #7: Becoming a Woman of Hope

Acknowledgments

Thank you to my precious family, Curt, Grace, and Joy, for your encouragement, love, and support. Thank you to my dad, Garry Kinder. Your positive words and example have been a powerful influence in my life.

Thank you to my dear friends and my sweet sister for your prayers, stories, and advice.

Thank you to Howard Publishing for your continued excellence in producing quality Christian literature.

"Now to Him who is able to keep you from stumbling, and to make you stand in the presence of His glory blameless with great joy, to the only God our Savior, through Jesus Christ our Lord, be glory, majesty, dominion and authority, before all time and now and forever" (Jude 24–25 NASB).

How wonderful is it that nobody need wait a single moment before starting to improve the world?

—Anne Frank

Introduction

The Great Adventure
Living Life As an Expression of God Within

Live a life full of steady enthusiasm.

—Florence Nightingale

Are you a positive woman? By that I mean, do you want to move in a positive direction and make a lasting, positive impact in the lives of the people around you?

Often we think that a positive woman is a perky woman with a perfect life. But I'm going to let you in on a little secret: *I'm not always perky, and my life circumstances are far from perfect.* (I know that's your little secret too. Don't worry; I won't tell anyone.) The good news is we don't have to be perfect, because we have a perfect God who can use even our imperfections in an eternal, powerful, and positive way. We can be positive women simply by choosing to allow God's power and strength to pour through us. We can choose to see God's hand at work in our lives and in the circumstances around us.

Recently I ran across something called "The Ten Commandments for an Unhappy Life." It serves as a humorous reminder of the choices we face every single day: Will we enjoy the gifts and challenges life brings, or will we grumble and be miserable through the process? Will we be women of wonder or women of woe?

The Ten Commandments for an Unhappy Life

1. Thou shalt hold onto bitterness and anger.

2. Thou shalt never get too close to anybody. Keepeth all of thy relationships at surface level.

3. Thou shalt wear a glum expression on thy face at all times.

4. Thou shalt put aside play and shalt inflict upon others that which was once inflicted upon thyself.

5. Thou shalt grumble about the small stuff, forgetting the bigger picture.

6. Thou shalt forget about others' needs, thinking only of your own.

7. Thou shalt hold regular pity parties, inviting others to joinest thou.

8. Thou shalt not take a vacation.

9. Thou shalt expect the worst in all situations, blame and shame everyone around thyself for everything, and dwell on the feebleness, faults, and fears of others.

10. Thou shalt be in control at all times, no matter what.[1]

I don't know about you, but in the great adventure of life, I want to experience joy in the journey—not misery in the muck! I want my life to move in a positive direction. And since you're reading this book, I think you do too.

In the chapters that follow we will explore seven principles that, if applied, can make us positive women—women moving in a positive direction and having a positive impact on our families, our communities, our churches, and our world. These are powerful principles because they are *biblical* principles. In addition to finding delightful quotes, wonderful Bible passages, and motivating messages designed to encourage and strengthen you, you will read true stories of women who have exemplified these principles in their lives. Some stories are from the Bible, while other stories are about famous women from history or the current day. Some are about little-known women who have experienced God's strength in a mighty way and stand as living examples to us all.

Each chapter closes with a Power Point section that allows you to use this book for your own personal growth or for a study with other women in your church or neighborhood. In each Power Point you will find a Bible passage to read and several questions to ponder. Don't miss this opportunity! As great as it is to read a book, I believe it's even better to ponder the implications and reflect on the ideas presented in the text. When I was growing up, one of my favorite Sunday school teachers lived at a unique intersection in Dallas: at the corner of two streets named Pensive and Ponder. I think we should all live at the corner of Pensive and Ponder, figuratively speaking. We need to take the time to ponder and reflect upon God's wonderful words to us.

Each Power Point also includes a suggested Bible verse to place in your heart or memorize. (A simple plan for memorizing scripture is presented in chapter 5.) It also has an action plan to stimulate you to apply and put "feet" on what you have just learned. I'm sure you will find these applications simple yet helpful and even fun. This book is meant to be an energy boost for your spirit. It is a quick read with deep truths. It can be a lifestyle changer, if you'll let it.

Perhaps you're asking, "Can any woman be a positive woman? Can someone who tends to be negative, fearful, or unhappy change her attitude and perspective on life?" Yes! Yes! Yes! Every woman has the potential to be a positive woman, because each of us has the opportunity to invite God to work in our lives. We have the choice to

His divine power has given us everything we need for life and godliness through our knowledge of him who called us by his own glory and goodness. —2 Peter 1:3

look to a wonderful heavenly Father and seek his salvation, power, and strength. After all, the qualities of a positive woman are ultimately the qualities of our awesome God. As God works in us and through us, he is able to conform us to his image. And that's the key: It's his work in us, not our own.

The psalmist recognized the positive qualities of God when he declared:

> Praise the LORD, O my soul; all my inmost being, praise his holy name. Praise the LORD, O my soul, and forget not all his benefits—who forgives all your sins and heals all your diseases, who redeems your life from the pit and crowns you with love and compassion, who satisfies your desires with good things so that your youth is renewed like the eagle's.
>
> The LORD works righteousness and justice for all the oppressed....The LORD is compassionate and gracious, slow to anger, abounding in love. He will not always accuse, nor will he harbor his anger forever; he does not treat us as our sins deserve or repay us according to our iniquities. For as high as the heavens are above the earth, so great is his love for those who fear him; as far as the east is from the west, so far has he removed our transgressions from us. (Psalm 103:1–12)

Isn't our heavenly Father wonderful? His desire is to love and forgive us, to be gracious to us. He lifts our lives out of the pit of our circumstances and crowns us with love and compassion. He lovingly teaches us how to live according to his righteousness. He doesn't hold grudges. He is slow to anger. He satisfies and renews our spirits.

As God's children, we have a reason to be enthusiastic about life! I love that word, *enthusiasm*. We tend to think of enthusiasm as excitement or passion, but its original meaning is "supernatural inspiration or possession by God." It actually comes from two Greek words, *en theos*—literally, "God within." By definition, then, all Christians should be automatically enthusiastic!

But is that what the people around us see? Can they see our enthusiasm? Can they see God within us?

Given the fear, grief, and turmoil that dominates our world (particularly since the events of September 11), there has never been a more important time for the love of God to shine through positive women. If you and I will choose to live life as an enthusiastic expression of the God who lives within us, we will become beacons that shine forth love, faith, wisdom, prayer, joy, courage, and hope in a world that desperately needs each of these qualities. We will have a powerful, positive impact for Christ in our homes, our communities, and beyond.

Never underestimate the power of a positive woman. And that woman can be you!

Portrait of a Positive Woman

Light tomorrow with today.

—Elizabeth Barrett Browning

May our Lord Jesus Christ himself and God our Father,
who loved us and by his grace gave us eternal encouragement
and good hope, encourage your hearts and
strengthen you in every good deed and word.

—2 Thessalonians 2:16–17

It's a Girl Thing
Relishing the Unique Qualities of a Woman

I praise you because I am fearfully and wonderfully made;
your works are wonderful, I know that full well.

—Psalm 139:14

Let's play a quick game of Jeopardy. What do the following activities have in common?

- Spending an hour and a half looking at tools in a hardware store.

- Playing thirty-six holes of golf in 103-degree weather.

- Sitting on metal chairs in freezing temperatures watching men beat each other up over a little brown ball.

- Using the remote control to switch to seventeen different stations in less than ten seconds.

- Getting angry when the remote is lost or strategically misplaced.

- Fishing for hours while saying a total of five words the entire time.

If your answer is "What activities do guys typically enjoy?" you're right! Can you believe so many men actually think those activities are fun? I'd rather have my teeth pulled—at least the dentist shoots you full of Novocaine so you can't feel the pain! While it's hard for us to comprehend why anyone would enjoy lying on the frozen ground at the break of dawn to hunt snow geese, men, on the other hand, cannot fathom why women would want to:

- Stroll from one end of a shopping mall to the other in search of the perfect shoes.

- Share favorite recipes over a cup of mocha java.

- Cry at romantic movies.

- Talk for hours about…

- Decorate scrapbooks together until the wee hours of the night.

- Join a garden club, book club, or Bunko group.

- Go to the rest room after dinner in pairs.

- Refresh makeup and hair every three hours.

- Have more than five pairs of black shoes.

I suppose there is a chasm of understanding between the sexes that's just too great to bridge. Even in early childhood the differences between boys and girls are obvious. I'll never forget the time I took my young daughters to see Disney's *Little Mermaid* at the theater. For some unknown reason, the movie projector malfunctioned. The manager came into the auditorium and announced that it would take about fifteen minutes to fix the problem.

As the lights went on, the little girls in the theater sat nicely in their seats and waited patiently for the movie to resume. Not the little boys! They immediately began to fill the aisles—running, playing, and forcing their mothers to chase them. Every child in the aisles was a boy (with the exception of one girl who was being chased by her brother). It was one of those hilarious moments in the observation of human nature—and a glaring example of the innate differences in the behavior and interests of boys and girls. I must admit a thought of gratitude bolted through my mind as I watched some of the frazzled mothers: *Thank you, Lord, for giving me girls!*

The differences, of course, don't end with childhood. In our home my husband, Curt, and I represent two perspectives. Curt's idea of a perfect weeknight evening is eating a home-cooked meal, inviting friends over for dessert, and sitting around talking for hours. My idea of a perfect weeknight evening is eating out at a quiet restaurant; successfully helping the kids with their homework (no griping); then curling up with a good book, a chocolate brownie, and a glass of milk while listening to soothing classical music. (Of course, this second scenario has never actually happened—but I can always dream!)

When it comes to vacations, Curt's ideal adventure would be to charter a sailboat in the Caribbean. We would man the boat along with a hired captain and visit the islands of our choice—each with a golf course on which he would play. My ideal vacation would be on a luxury cruise liner (with large master suites and gourmet food) that would visit five or six islands with the sole purpose of shopping and sunning at each.

Needless to say, Curt and I both have to make a few compromises in our relationship. But our marriage is as strong and as whole as it is today because we blend together our unique qualities and interests. We balance each other out. That's how it is in marriage and in life: God uses the differing gifts, talents, strengths, and weaknesses of men and women to make this world a better place.

I say: Let's celebrate the differences! Let's embrace our uniqueness as women, recognizing that we were created with distinctly feminine characteristics.

Distinctly Feminine

Take a moment to think how you would define a woman. Webster's dictionary defines *woman* as "an adult female person, as distinguished from a girl or a man." I'm sorry, but I think Webster missed a few important distinctions! My definition would include descriptive words such as nurturing, kind, loving, graceful, gracious, intuitive, strong, wise, creative, resourceful, sensitive, caring, courageous, and determined. What words would you add to that definition?

From Eve to Mary to Mother Teresa, God has had a unique plan for women on this earth. He created us with his own definition in mind, using our womanly strengths as well as some of our female flaws to paint an eternal picture.

Consider the beautiful and purposeful creation of the first woman, Eve. In a fascinating passage from Genesis 2, we read: "The LORD God said, 'It is not good for the man to be alone. I will make a helper suitable for him'" (Genesis 2:18). Oddly enough, all the things God had created up to that point had been declared "good." Light, water, atmosphere, vegetation, animals—they were all good. The first man, Adam, communed with God in a perfect garden paradise. Seems as though God could have stopped there. But it was not good that man was alone. God in his wisdom knew that Adam needed a completer, a helper. The world needed a woman's touch.

Verses 21–22 say, "So the LORD God caused the man to fall into a deep sleep; and while he was sleeping, he took one of the man's ribs and closed up the place with flesh. Then the LORD God made a woman from the rib he had taken out of the man, and he brought her to the man." Don't you find it interesting that God didn't form woman from the dust of the ground, as he did man and beast? No, woman was formed from man's side, demonstrating our commonality with men as human beings and yet our unique and separate creation as females.

It is fascinating to note what the Bible says about human beings as opposed to other life forms. Genesis 1:27 tells us mankind was created in God's own image. Male and female alike bear the image and likeness of God. But while you and I were created in the likeness of God, we are not *exactly* like God. Only Christ himself is "the exact representation of his being" (Hebrews 1:3). So how do we humans bear our Creator's likeness? Matthew Henry's *Commentary on the Whole Bible* points out three distinct areas:

The soul. Generally the term *soul* refers to the will, understanding, and active power found within each individual. The soul is the intelligent, immortal spirit within us.

Place and authority. Genesis 1:26 tells us that men and women have dominion or rule over all living things—that we are God's representatives for governing the Earth's lower creatures. That is our role and place of authority in this world. We also have authority over ourselves in that we have been given a free will. We have the right to make choices. What a profound gift from God!

Purity and moral virtue. At first I didn't agree with Matthew Henry on this one. As I read on, however, I began to grasp what he was saying. Before sin entered the world, Adam and Eve saw divine things clearly. Their wills complied readily and universally to the will of God, without reluctance or resistance. The first man and woman were holy and happy as they bore the image of God upon them! It's sad to think about our origin as God's image-bearers and realize the ruin sin has had upon it. Since the Fall we've been corrupt in nature—but thankfully we can put on a new self in Christ.[1]

God formed Eve, the mother of humanity, in his image and according to his perfect design. Like Adam, she had a soul; she was given a place of dominion and authority; and she reflected God's purity and moral virtue. Was she perfect? No; in fact, she was the first to succumb to temptation. But God used both her strengths and her weaknesses for an eternal purpose.

God created each of us in his image as well. Oh that we would value his creation more as we deal with others—and as we deal with ourselves! Let's hold dear the fact that we are wonderfully made by him. And let's relish the heritage we have as specially fashioned creatures designed for a unique plan and purpose in this world.

Created with a Purpose

Within the Bible and throughout history we can read about the women God has used to accomplish his purposes—some in big ways, others in seemingly small ways. All with individual strengths, all with personal weaknesses. Each with a divine purpose. Why didn't God just use men to accomplish his work? Because some purposes required the unique feminine qualities that he placed in women alone.

Let's take a brief carriage ride through history and meet some of the women who exemplified qualities that God used in great and lasting ways.

Courage. According to Edith Deen's *All the Women of the Bible,* Deborah was "the only woman in the Bible who was placed at the height of political power by the common consent of the people."[2] Deborah's courage, like that of Joan of Arc twenty-seven centuries later, was based on her faith in the LORD. She was a counselor, a judge, and a deliverer in time of war. When other leaders were afraid, she led the nation of Israel into battle and on to victory with these words: "Go! This is the day the LORD has given Sisera into your hands. Has not the LORD gone ahead of you?" (Judges 4:14). Deborah's story is told in greater detail when we look at women of courage in chapter 13.

Loyalty. Ruth is the picture of enduring loyalty in unfavorable circumstances. When her Jewish husband died and she was free to go back to her own people, she chose to stay with her mother-in-law, Naomi, and follow the God of Israel. From Ruth we have the oft-quoted statement "Where you go I will go, and where you stay I will stay. Your people will be my people and your God my God" (Ruth 1:16).

Through her loyalty to Naomi she met Boaz, whom she later married, and had a son, Obed—grandfather of King David and a member of the lineage of Christ!

Beauty. Esther's beauty saved her people! When the king was searching for a new queen, Esther entered the royal beauty contest and won. But Esther had much more than surface beauty; she exhibited strength, courage, patience, wisdom, and faith. When a decree went out that all Israelites would be killed, Esther bravely went before the king, wisely invited him to a series of banquets, and carefully chose her moment to plead their case. Her actions resulted in the saving of the Jewish people, and to this day they celebrate this victory.

Purity of heart. "Do not be afraid, Mary, you have found favor with God," the angel told the woman who would become the mother of Jesus (Luke 1:30). Humble and pure, Mary was highly favored among women as God's chosen vessel to bring his Son into the world. Her response to Gabriel reveals her precious spirit: "I am the Lord's servant. May it be to me as you have said" (Luke 1:38). Her heart was ready to serve God, and she was prepared for the great work he would accomplish through her life. In her song of praise to God, we again see that purity of heart: "My soul glorifies the Lord and my spirit rejoices in God my Savior, for he has been mindful of the humble state of his servant. From now on all generations will call me blessed, for the Mighty One has done great things for me—holy is his name" (Luke 1:46–49).

Organization. As the mother of nineteen children, Susannah Wesley (1669–1742) realized the importance of staying organized. She dedicated her children to God and made a point of spending individual time with each one each day. Her "Thirteen Rules of Child Rearing" are as applicable today as they were over two hundred years ago.[3] Because of her nurturing and caring heart, combined with organization and discipline, her children went on to make an eternal difference in

15

this world. Perhaps you recognize two of their names: John and Charles Wesley.

Creativity. Emily Dickinson (1830–1886) is recognized as one of the greatest poets of the nineteenth century. Peggy Anderson writes of her in *Great Quotes from Great Women,* "Emily Dickinson lived intensely, finding in her books, her garden, and friends the possibilities of rich experience and fulfillment."[4] After Emily's death, over a thousand poems were discovered in her desk. She is estimated to have written a total of more than eighteen hundred poems, several hundred of which are considered to be among the finest ever composed by an American poet. Oddly enough, only a small number were published during her lifetime. Yet Emily's gift remains with us to this day, as she says in her own words: "The poet lights the light and fades away. But the light goes on and on."

Leadership. Born in 1820 as a slave in Maryland, Harriet Tubman escaped to Pennsylvania and to freedom in 1849. She earned enough money to return to the South and led her sister and her two children to freedom. Carrying a long rifle, she continued making trips back and forth from the South to the North, leading an estimated three hundred people to freedom along the secret network of safe houses dubbed the "Underground Railroad." She became known as "Moses" to her people as she led them out of slavery to a better place.

After the Civil War, Harriet opened a home for the aged and raised funds for schools for former slaves. She later worked with her friend Susan B. Anthony in the New England Suffrage Association. The impact of her love, courage, and leadership remains an example for us all.

Resourcefulness. During her high school years, Fannie Farmer (1857–1915) suffered paralysis from a stroke, causing her to discontinue her education. After her recovery she worked as a "mother's helper" and acquired a keen interest in cooking. Resourceful and determined, she went on to study cooking at the Boston Cooking School, where she eventually became the director. She was the first person to institute the use of exact measurements in recipes, thereby guaranteeing more reliable results. In her lifetime she wrote numerous books and opened her own cooking school. Certainly all women can thank Miss Farmer for her lasting contribution to the science of cooking!

Compassion. Clara Barton was known as the "Angel of the Battlefield" during the Civil War. She established several free schools during the war and organized her own band of volunteers to distribute supplies to the battlefields, often driving a four-mule wagon team into the fields herself. After the war she set up a records bureau to help families searching for missing soldiers.

Later Clara founded a military hospital in Europe during the Franco-Prussian War and was decorated with the Iron Cross for her services. It was in Europe that she first learned about the International Red Cross, inspiring her to organize an American branch in 1881. Today more than one million American Red Cross volunteers help millions of people each year.

Nurture. The entire world has been touched by the brilliance of Thomas Alva Edison, born in 1847, to whom is credited the incandescent lamp, phonograph, and microphone, among numerous other inventions. But few people realize the impact his mother made on his life. Although his teachers and classmates considered him a dunce, his mother believed in him to the point of taking him out of school and teaching him herself. Under her tutelage, he was allowed to work on experiments down in the cellar to his heart's content.

Many years later he had this to say about his mother's nurturing spirit: "I did not have my mother long, but she cast over me an influence which has lasted all my life. The good effects of her early training I can never lose. If it had not been for her appreciation and her faith in

God has a history of using the insignificant to accomplish the impossible. —Richard Exley

17

me at a critical time in my experience, I should never likely have become an inventor. I was always a careless boy, and with a mother of different mental caliber, I should have turned out badly. But her firmness, her sweetness, her goodness were potent powers to keep me in the right path. My mother was the making of me."[5]

Perseverance. Helen Keller showed us how to persevere and overcome great odds. Born in 1880, a severe illness left her unable to see or hear. But through the patient and persistent instruction of her teacher, Anne Sullivan, Helen went on to learn to read, write, and speak. She studied French and Greek at Radcliffe College and graduated in 1904. At the age of twenty-six she published her life story and became a well-known public figure and humanitarian. In her lifetime she lectured in over twenty-five countries and received several awards of great distinction. "It gives me a deep, comforting sense that things seen are temporal and things unseen are eternal."[6] Certainly her incredible accomplishments epitomize human potential in the face of adversity.

Mental fortitude. Marie Curie was a Polish-born French scientist who, along with her husband, Pierre, experimented extensively with uranium radiation. In 1903 the couple shared the Nobel Prize for physics with Henri Becquerel, making Marie the first woman to receive the Nobel Prize. After Pierre's death in 1906, Marie continued her research and succeeded her husband as a professor of physics at the University of Paris. In 1911 she received a second Nobel Prize in chemistry, making her the first person to receive two Nobel Prizes. Not only were her discoveries helpful to mankind, but her example laid the groundwork for women in the field of science.

Determination. Amelia Earhart was the first woman to fly solo across the Atlantic Ocean. She first took up aviation as a hobby, and after a series of record flights, she made a solo transatlantic flight from Harbour Grace, Newfoundland, to Ireland. In 1937 she attempted the first round-the-world flight traveling close to the equator. She took off on July 1 from New Guinea headed toward Howland Island in the Pacific, but her plane vanished. A naval search found nothing, and it was eventually decided that she had been lost at sea. Although her death was a mystery, her courage and determination were unquestioned.

Physical strength. Mildred "Babe" Didrickson Zaharias was named "the greatest woman athlete of the first half of the twentieth century" by the Associated Press in 1950. During her high school years she excelled in basketball, which led to playing sports in the Amateur Athletics Union (AAU). She later took up track and field and again excelled, winning gold medals in javelin and 80-meter hurdles and a silver medal in high jump in the 1932 Olympic Games. Next Babe took up golf, winning an unprecedented seventeen consecutive golf tournaments and becoming the first American to win the Women's British Open. Her success helped to open the door for women athletes in a wide variety of professional sports.[7]

Love. Mother Teresa devoted her life to working with the impoverished people of India. In 1948, through the leading of God, she began the order of the Missionaries of Charity. The sisters of the order serve as nurses and social workers, sharing Christ's love with the poor and the sick. In 1952 Mother Teresa opened the Nirmal Hriday (Pure Heart) Home for Dying Destitutes in Calcutta. She was awarded the Nobel Peace Prize in 1975 and the Presidential Medal of Freedom from the United States in 1985. Her selfless commitment to helping the poor touched nearly eight thousand people in Calcutta alone—not to mention all the rest of us who've been encouraged by her example of selfless, unconditional love.

Encouragement. In the early 1960s, Mary Kay Ash courageously invested her life savings to establish a cosmetics company that ended up revolutionizing the confidence and careers of hundreds of thousands of women. She is best known for her creed: "God first, family second, career third." Her loving encouragement gave the women who joined her company the power to reach their full potential as talented and successful individuals. She gave women hope, encouraged their faith, strengthened their confidence, and changed many lives. You can read more about Mary Kay's story in chapter 4.

Graciousness. It would be impossible to name all of the gracious ladies who have blessed this world with their kindness, hospitality, and sense of honor. Many come to mind, but one stands out in our day: Barbara Bush. As the wife of former President George Bush and mother of current President George W. Bush, her graciousness and steady influence have made an impact on the people of America over recent decades. Whether she is receiving foreign diplomats or reading to schoolchildren, Barbara's positive and gracious spirit continues to inspire us all.

Intuition. Victoria Cross Kelly is the deputy director of the PATH train system, which transports commuters between New York and New Jersey. On the morning of September 11, 2001, just minutes after the first World Trade Center tower was hit by the hijacked airliner, Kelly made the split-second decision to halt all discharge of passengers at the station underneath the Trade Center buildings. By 9:06 A.M. a rescue train had swept through the station one last time, collecting the last of the PATH workers and a homeless man who had to be coaxed onto the car. It was the last train ever to enter the World Trade Center station. Both towers had collapsed by 10:29.

It is estimated that Kelly's keen intuition and quick decision making saved three thousand to five thousand people. She admits that if her intuition had been wrong, "a heck of a lot of people would've been annoyed." But she wasn't wrong—and thousands of people are alive today because of her wise decision.[8]

You're an Original

As I look back on the lives of the women we've listed here, I think, *What a wonderful ride through history!* Our world is a better place because of the unique gifts and talents of such special females. And there are many more names we could add to the list. Untold millions of women have made a positive impact in their lifetimes—some famous, others not so well known. Yet each had a plan and a purpose in this world. Isn't it wonderful to know that God created you and me for a plan and a purpose as well?

Ephesians 2:10 says, "We are God's workmanship, created in Christ Jesus to do good works, which God prepared in advance for us to do." Dear sister, relish the thought that you are God's specially formed workmanship, designed by a perfect Creator and loving Father. You wear a designer label embossed with God's own fingerprint. And you were created to do good works that God has prepared especially for you. May you use the unique gifts, talents, and abilities he has given you to honor him, remembering that you, like me and like the women down through history, are a designer original!

POWER POINT

Read: Luke 8:3; John 20:10–18; Romans 16:1–2; 2 Timothy 1:5. Write down the names of the women mentioned in these passages and tell how God used them in unique ways.

Pray: Wonderful Creator, loving Father, faithful Lord, I praise you for your magnificent character. You are all-wise and all-powerful. Thank you for the wisdom and creativity you used as you fashioned me. Thank you for the unique qualities you have given women in general, and thank you for the characteristics you have specifically given to me. May I honor and glorify you with these gifts, talents, and capabilities. Thank you for the way you have used women throughout the ages. Please use me now to make a positive and eternal impact in this world. In Jesus' name, amen.

💡 **Remember:** "I praise you because I am fearfully and wonderfully made; your works are wonderful, I know that full well" (Psalm 139:14).

☺ **Do:** What is unique about you? Name some of the qualities and gifts God has given to you. (Don't say you can't think of anything—we both know there is something special about you!) In what ways can God use your strengths for a greater purpose? Make a list and dream big!

As you do this, consider the fact that God can take a small acorn and make it into a towering tree. And remember, "big" can mean many things. For you "big" may mean leading a company, teaching the Bible to a group of women, or making a difference in the life of one person. What seems small in the world's eyes may be big in the eternal scheme of things.

A Perfect Fit
Discovering Your Source of Power and Strength

*Many a humble soul will be amazed to find that the seed
it sowed in weakness, in the dust of daily life,
has blossomed into immortal flowers under the eye of the Lord.*

—Harriet Beecher Stowe

When shopping for clothes, I never pay full price. Pantyhose are no exception. After all, name-brand pantyhose are available at discount stores for a fraction of the cost of department stores with only one stipulation: The package is marked "slightly imperfect." Despite that marking, I have never had a problem with quality in the fifteen years I have been buying discounted hose. They have always been perfect for me.

Well, almost always. You know as well as I do that the inevitable was sure to happen—but did it have to happen when I was running late to an important high-society fashion show?

Several months ago I was scheduled to join a friend at Neiman Marcus for a fashion show featuring the best-dressed women in Dallas. In my hurry and fury to get ready, I pulled out my special-purchase pantyhose and immediately became aware that this pair was definitely less than perfect. My first indication was the fact that one leg was five inches longer than the other. Upon further examination, I realized that both legs of the hose were more than four feet long. Being only five-feet three-inches tall from head to toe, I quickly perceived that the legs were much too long for my build. I checked the box to make sure I had bought the right size, and I had. Nevertheless, these pantyhose weren't just too long for me—I think they would have been slightly too long for Andre the Giant! Inspector Number 11 must have been on her coffee break when these hose passed through her station.

"Slightly imperfect" was an understatement. These were uneven, overstretched, obviously imperfect pantyhose. I looked at them and laughed, remembering a time when I heard Florence Littauer talk about personality types. She held up a pair of pantyhose that had been labeled "slightly imperfect." Her pair had three legs! She related the hose to how we often feel slightly imperfect as people.

Would it be too much of a stretch (no pun intended) to say that I can relate to my pair of pantyhose? You see, I often feel overstretched, unbalanced, and obviously imperfect. As a friend, as a mother, as a spouse, in my work, at my church, at board meetings, I often feel as though I don't measure up to people's expectations, whether perceived or real. What about you? Is your package marked "imperfect" too?

The problem is bigger than any of us. Life isn't perfect. Circumstances aren't perfect. And people aren't perfect. But the good news is that God is a perfect fit for our overstretched, out of balance, more-than-slightly imperfect lives. He is able to make up for our imperfections and give us the strength and support we need.

If we want to experience the power of being positive women, we must fill our lives with the perfect power source. Some women believe their source of strength comes from within themselves, and certainly as women we have certain innate abilities; but in our own strength alone we will always fall short. God is our only reliable source of strength and power if we want to accomplish great and mighty things that have eternal value. As the apostle Paul said, "Christ in you" is "the hope of glory" (Colossians 1:27).

It's easy for us to put our hope in ourselves. But the Bible says the Lord delights in those who fear him and put their hope in him. Psalm 147:10–11 tells us, "His pleasure is not in the strength of the horse, nor his delight in the legs of a man; the LORD delights in those who fear him, who put their hope in his unfailing love." Over and over again, the psalmist declares that his own strength comes from the Lord. "The LORD is the stronghold [strength] of my life," he writes in Psalm 27:1 and elsewhere.

As Jesus drew near to his death, he gave his disciples a colorful illustration of God doing his work in and through them. His word picture was of a grapevine, a common plant and an important commodity in the region. Jesus said, "I am the vine; you are the branches. If a man remains in me and I in him, he will bear much fruit; apart from me you can do nothing" (John 15:5).

According to Jesus, our job is not to strive to achieve an abundant and fruitful life in our own strength. Our job is simply to remain in Christ. The words *remain in* mean to "dwell, abide, fellowship, and continue in" him. As we abide in him and he abides in us, he provides the strength, guidance, direction, and ability we need to "bear much fruit." How do we abide in him? By dwelling on his Word, remaining in his love, praying, and practicing his presence throughout the day. In subsequent chapters we will explore many wonderful ways to do each of these things.

Right now we need to ask ourselves: Is God our stronghold, or are we depending on our own strength and power to live our lives? If we want to be positive women, we must look daily to our heavenly Father for strength, support, and direction. He is more than able to work in us and through us, despite our imperfections.

Control Top or Sheer-to-Toe?

"Oh, I'm just a control freak." Have you noticed that more and more women seem to be making that confession? I'm not sure if we're getting better at recognizing and admitting our challenges, or if our hard-driving, Type-A culture is creating more people with control issues.

Of course, the desire to be in control is an age-old problem. Satan himself wanted to be like God, in authority over everything. And then there were the Pharisees. Talk about control freaks! They loaded so many rules and regulations on the Jewish people that Jesus was prompted to speak severely against them. In Matthew 23:4–5 he condemned the Pharisees, saying, "They tie up heavy loads [referring to the rules] and put them on men's shoulders, but they themselves are not willing to lift a finger to move them. Everything they do is done for men to see."

I think most of us want to be in control. But what is it that we want to control, and why do we want to control it? I can answer the first question in two words: *people* and *circumstances.* (That covers quite a bit of territory, don't you think?) Many times we want to make and mold people to fit inside our personal box of expectations. We want to control circumstances so that life will be smooth and easy and safe.

Certainly, we should not allow people to run over us, nor should we allow circumstances to run away with our lives. But neither should we demand to hold everything so tightly. We need to maintain a healthy balance in our lives by releasing those things we were never meant to control in the first place! We need to pry our grimy little hands off of the things that only God can control and look to his strength and power to take care of them.

Taking Matters into Her Own Hands

In the Old Testament, Sarai (later called Sarah) seemed to have a slight control issue. Let's begin her story by taking a brief look at Genesis 15. In a vision God told Abram, Sarai's husband, that he would have a son who would be his heir and that his descendants would be as numerous as the stars in the sky. At this point in the story, God didn't give the exact details on how this would be accomplished; he simply provided a plan with a promise.

By Genesis 16 some time had passed, the promised son had not arrived, and Sarai was itching to take matters into her own hands. From the beginning she'd had a twinge of doubt about her ability to have a baby. Now she told Abram, "The LORD has kept me from having children" (Genesis 16:2)—implying that God had not kept his promise.

We can't be too hard on Sarai. It's probably safe to assume that she had hoped and prayed for a child for years. Now she was far past the normal childbearing years. Her hope had dwindled, and her faith was tender. She had waited so long—and now the situation seemed hopeless. (Been there?) So to solve the problem herself, Sarai offered her maidservant, Hagar, to Abram, expecting Hagar to conceive and bear a child with her husband. It sounds strange to us today, I know, but Sarai was actually carrying out an ancient custom in Assyrian marriage contracts designed to ensure a male heir to a family.

It's so easy for us to turn to cultural, quick-fix solutions to our problems instead of waiting on the Lord! In our hurry-up, fast-track world, we tend to want solutions, and we want them *now*. Have you ever pleaded with God that your husband would change in a certain area, and when immediate changes didn't occur, you took on the job of "holy nudger"? Perhaps you prayed for a situation at work to get better, but when you didn't see quick results, you felt as though God had not heard your cry. Sometimes waiting on the Lord can be the hardest thing to do! But Psalm 27:14 encourages us: "Wait for the LORD; be strong and take heart and wait for the LORD."

Quick solutions rarely bring the best results. (In Sarai's case, the ramifications of her quick-fix decision are still seen in the turmoil in

My grace is sufficient for you, for my power is made perfect in weakness. —2 Corinthians 12:9

☺

the Middle East today.) Immediate gratification can rob us of joys to be received or lessons to be learned from God's deeper, more thorough plan. Remember, God sees the whole picture from a heavenly viewpoint; we only see the narrow situation right before our eyes. Isaiah 55:8–9 reminds us of God's eternal perspective and our own lack of sight: "'For my thoughts are not your thoughts, neither are your ways my ways,' declares the LORD. 'As the heavens are higher than the earth, so are my ways higher than your ways and my thoughts than your thoughts.'" These faith-building words help us recognize that we don't understand everything—but God does.

When faced with a problem, each of us must ask ourselves: Are we willing to trust God's Word and allow his purpose to be worked out in our lives? Or are we going to jump in and try to fix things ourselves? As Isaiah 55 makes clear, God understands our situation much better than we do. We're probably not the best ones to be calling the shots!

Let's rejoin Abram and Sarai and see how God's plan continued to unfold for them. In Genesis 17 God spoke again to Abram, this time telling him specifically that Sarai would have a son and that the covenant promise would be through this son. Interestingly, God also changed Abram's name to Abraham and Sarai's name to Sarah at this point. Both Sarai and Sarah mean "princess." But in announcing Sarah's new name, God added these words: "I will bless her and will surely give you [Abraham] a son by her" (Genesis 17:16)—thus making her name both royal and rich with promise.

In Genesis 18 God assured the couple once again that Sarah would have a son. But watch Sarah's response:

Then the LORD said, "I will surely return to you about this time next year, and Sarah your wife will have a son." Now Sarah was listening at the entrance to the tent, which was behind him. Abraham and Sarah were already old and well advanced in years, and Sarah was past the age of childbearing. So Sarah laughed to herself as she thought, "After I am worn out and my master is old, will I now have this pleasure?"

Then the LORD said to Abraham, "Why did Sarah laugh and say, 'Will I really have a child, now that I am old?' Is there anything too hard for the LORD? I will return to you at the appointed time next year and Sarah will have a son."

Sarah was afraid, so she lied and said, "I did not laugh."

But he said, "Yes, you did laugh." (Genesis 18:10–15)

I have to chuckle a little at the "No I didn't; yes you did" episode, but don't we all have times when we want to hide our shortcomings? Who are we trying to fool? God sees everything, so we might as well confess! In Sarah's case, when God made it clear that his plan was for her to have a baby, she laughed to herself—but God heard her. He recognized her lack of faith, yet loved her through her doubt. "Is anything too hard for the LORD?" he asked in Genesis 18:14, reminding both Abraham and Sarah that with God, nothing is impossible.

The truth is, our need to be in control of a person or a situation is most often a reflection of our lack of faith in God to protect us, lead us, and provide for us in his timing. Are you struggling with doubt? Worried about the future? Perhaps you are having trouble with a relationship. Maybe you feel as though you will never see victory over a sin that has gripped you. Take comfort in the fact that nothing is too hard for God! Trust him with your greatest longings, your deepest needs, and your strongest doubts. He is with you, and he sees far beyond what you see.

Whether God's plan is clear to us or still a bit sketchy, we need to lay down the control panel and let him navigate. But we must not misunderstand what it means to give God control of our lives. It doesn't mean we have no responsibilities or decisions to make. We still must act upon our duties and respond to the opportunities he sets before us. Giving God control doesn't mean that we sit back and do nothing; it means that we move forward in wisdom, let go of the need to control or hurry the process, and trust God to do his divine work.

Fits Like a Glove

One time Corrie ten Boom held up a common, white ladies' glove to her audience and asked the question, "What can a glove do?" She went on to remind her listeners of the power and influence a woman can have if she relies on God for her strength:

> The glove can do nothing. Oh but if my hand is in the glove, it can do many things…cook, play the piano, write. Well, you say that is not the glove, that is the hand in the glove that does it. Yes, that is so. I tell you that we are nothing but gloves. The hand in the glove is the Holy Spirit of God. Can the glove do something if it is very near the hand? No! The glove must be filled with the hand to do the work. That is exactly the same for us: We must be filled with the Holy Spirit to do the work God has for us to do.[1]

Oh, dear friends, we have a powerful God! Is anything too hard for him? And to think that we, as women who have chosen to follow Jesus, have his Spirit living within us! God's Spirit dwells in us, empowering us to live, to walk, and to achieve eternal tasks for his glory. Hear the words of Paul to the Christians in Rome: "But if Christ is in you, your body is dead because of sin, yet your spirit is alive because of righteousness. And if the Spirit of him who raised Jesus from the dead is living in you, he who raised Christ from the dead will also give life to your mortal bodies through his Spirit, who lives in you" (Romans 8:10–11).

Is that not simply amazing? Think about it: The same Spirit of him who raised Christ from the dead dwells within us! Paul was an incredibly powerful and influential apostle, yet he didn't hesitate to say, "For when I am weak, then I am strong" in Christ (2 Corinthians 12:10). He knew that Jesus is the perfect fit for our glove of human weakness, inability, and imperfection.

When I was a counselor at Pine Cove Camp in East Texas, one of my responsibilities was to serve as a lifeguard during the afternoon swimming sessions. In my official training course, I learned that one of the most difficult challenges for a rescuer is to assist swimmers who are struggling and hysterical. When victims are thrashing about in the water and trying desperately to stay afloat, they put the lifeguard in great danger of being pulled under with them. But if they release their struggle and relax in the safe hold of the lifeguard, then the lifeguard's strength can pull them to safety.

I like to picture our release to God in the same way. So often we struggle to solve life's battles in our own strength, and our efforts do nothing but wear us out and pull us under. But when we release our lives to God and trust that he holds us safely in the palm of his hand, we allow his strength and power to see us through.

What exactly does it mean to release our control to God? What does it mean to release our will, our strength, and our power to him? What does it look like on a daily basis? We're not talking about a month-by-month commitment or a year-to-year deal; we're talking about a daily commitment to submit to God's authority. Jesus told his disciples in Luke 9:23–24, "If anyone would come after me, he must deny himself and take up his cross daily and follow me. For whoever wants to save his life will lose it, but whoever loses his life for me will save it." Sounds a lot like the lifeguard situation, doesn't it?

Consider the scenario of two women—I'll call them Tonya and

Susan—each with daughters in kindergarten. Tonya's daughter was one of the younger kids in the class and struggled with several of the basic skills that would be needed for first grade. The teacher recommended that the little girl spend a year in a pre–first-grade class before moving up to the next grade level. Tonya became angry and upset at the idea; she didn't want her daughter to be held back while most of her little friends moved up to first grade.

Tonya never thought to pray about the situation. Instead she argued, complained, and forced the issue with the school administration. With misgivings the principal finally okayed her daughter's move to first grade. Unfortunately, the girl struggled in class the next year and fell behind the other students. She became defeated and discouraged—an attitude that ended up influencing her entire school career.

Meanwhile, Susan was also told that her daughter was not quite ready for first grade. Although Susan was a little surprised and saddened, she listened to what the teacher had to say about her daughter's lag in developmental skills. Over the next few weeks Susan studied the situation and collected pertinent information on child development and success in school. She also began to pray for wisdom and direction, recognizing that God knew exactly what was best for her daughter. She turned over to God any worry or need to control the situation.

In the end Susan decided to put her daughter in the pre–first-grade class for the next school year. Her decision was based on wise counsel, much thought, and faith-filled prayer. The class was, of course, a perfect fit! When her daughter eventually entered the first grade a year later, she was at the top of her class. Her success and sense of accomplishment positively colored the rest of her school experience.

How often do we hold on to an idea of what we think is best rather than resting in the safe care of the Lord? We need to remember that resting in the Lord—giving God the control panel—doesn't mean that

You can accomplish more in one hour with God than in one lifetime without Him.
—Quote from *God's Little Instruction Book for Women*

we stop doing what it takes to reach our goals. It means that we pray and actively trust God with our goals, our work, and the outcome. It means that as we move forward, we do so believing that he loves us and wants what's best for us. We know he sees a much bigger picture than we ever could.

Jars of Clay

Several years ago we bought a chiminea—a giant clay pot that sits on a stand outdoors. The chiminea has a large hole in the body of the pot and another opening in the top, making it the perfect receptacle in which to burn pinion wood. The wood is not burnt so much for warmth as it is for the wonderful, woodsy aroma it produces. It smells as though we are in Colorado. And since we're in Dallas, that's a treat! The scent can be picked up all over the neighborhood. Many times we will light the wood in the chiminea just before dinner guests arrive, and they consistently comment on the heavenly smell.

The Bible says that you and I are like clay pots. Look with me at 2 Corinthians 4:6–11:

> For God, who said, "Let light shine out of darkness," made his light shine in our hearts to give us the light of the knowledge of the glory of God in the face of Christ. But we have this treasure in jars of clay to show that this all-surpassing power is from God and not from us. We are hard pressed on every side, but not crushed; perplexed, but not in despair; persecuted, but not abandoned; struck down, but not destroyed. We always carry around in our body the death of Jesus, so that the life of Jesus may also be revealed in our body. For we who are alive are always being given over to death for Jesus' sake, so that his life may be revealed in our mortal body.

In Paul's time it was customary to hide personal treasure in clay jars. Because the pots were common and had little beauty or value, they didn't attract attention to themselves or to the precious contents contained therein. What a contrast—treasure in clay pots! Yet that describes us to a *T*. God's all-surpassing power and greatness is placed in common, frail, and unworthy containers known as men and women. Who would have guessed? Paul recognized his weaknesses; yet because of what was inside of him, he was able to move forward powerfully in God's strength. We can too.

Our lives in Christ are like that chiminea I mentioned a moment ago. The scent that permeates the environment, the light that pours forth into the darkness, and the warmth that dispels the cold are the result of the fire within us. God's power takes an unlikely yet willing receptacle and uses it in a mighty way.

Fanny Crosby was a perfect example of a chiminea for God. She was a woman who shined for Christ, allowing God's Spirit to light the world through her, even though her own life was darkened by blindness. Despite her handicap, Fanny wrote an estimated eight thousand gospel songs. Think about that staggering number! Not eighty songs, which would have been quite an accomplishment for anyone. Not eight hundred songs, which would have been a heroic feat. But an overwhelming *eight thousand* songs poured forth from this woman who had a heart for God and a willing hand to write. Given the physical obstacles she faced, we know that this was nothing short of miraculous!

Born into a humble household in Southeast, New York, in 1823, Fanny became blind at six weeks of age due to improper medical treatment. She was educated at the New York School for the Blind and eventually served as a teacher at the school. Her early writing was in secular verse; but through the influence of W. B. Bradbury, a popular church musician of the day, she began writing gospel song lyrics in her early forties, becoming, in her words, "the happiest creature in all the land."

Her gifting and her heart for God were obvious from an early age. When she was eight years old she wrote the following poem:

Oh, what a happy soul am I!
Although I cannot see,
I am resolved that in this world
Contented I will be.
How many blessings I enjoy
That other people don't;
To weep and sigh because I'm blind,
I cannot, and I won't.[2]

Fanny went on to write such well-known hymns as "Blessed Assurance," "All the Way My Savior Leads Me," "Rescue the Perishing," and "Saved by Grace." It has been said that she never wrote the lyrics to a hymn until she had first kneeled in earnest prayer and asked for God's guidance.

In his book *101 Hymn Stories,* Kenneth W. Osbeck notes that "Fanny J. Crosby died at the age of ninety-five. Only eternity will disclose the host of individuals who have been won to a saving faith in Jesus Christ or those whose lives have been spiritually enriched through the texts of her many hymns."[3] On her tombstone is engraved a simple verse: "She hath done what she could." Certainly she was a clay pot who allowed God's power to pour forth through her.

A Motley Crew

St. Augustine said, "Beware of despairing about yourself; you are commanded to put your trust in God, and not in yourself."[4] When I think about the twelve disciples Jesus chose to carry on his kingdom work, I think about what an unlikely group of people they were. Their band included several fishermen, a tax collector, a zealot, and some demanding brothers. They certainly were not trained in the finest schools in the country or prepared for great speaking careers. But God didn't call them to trust in their own abilities. He called them to trust in him. Through his power, direction, and strength, they were able to become Jesus' mouthpieces to spread the good news about the kingdom of God.

If God purposed to use this motley crew to spread the Gospel to the world, what can he do with willing vessels like you and me? The answer has nothing to do with our power and ability—and everything to do with his! What is your source of power and strength? Remember, God's Holy Spirit is at work in your life to accomplish the job he is calling you to do as a positive woman in this world. He's the fire in the pot, the hand in the glove. He's the perfect fit!

POWER POINT

⚙ **Read:** John 6:5–15, the story of Jesus feeding the five thousand. What did the little boy in this passage have to offer? What part did he have in the miracle? What part did God play? Notice how many people were blessed through this boy's willingness combined with God's power. What personal message do you think the disciples received from this experience?

♡ **Pray:** Dear Lord, Light of the world, I praise you for shining your light through me. I know that I am only a jar of clay in the Potter's hands. Help me to be a willing vessel and not an anxious or controlling woman. Mold me with your powerful touch. Fill me with your wonderful Spirit. Allow your work to be done in my life, using both my strengths and weaknesses for an eternal purpose. I trust you to faithfully lead me because you are my loving heavenly Father. In Jesus' name, amen.

💡 **Remember:** "Is anything too hard for the LORD?" (Genesis 18:14).

☺ **Do:** Set aside thirty minutes to an hour and spend some time alone with God for the specific purpose of releasing your life to him. Ask him to reveal areas where you tend to demand control. Release these areas to him one by one, asking for his power and strength to walk forward with him at the control panel of your life.

Power Principle #1

Becoming A Woman of Faith

Faith does not operate in the realm of the possible. There is no glory for God in that which is humanly possible. Faith begins where man's power ends.
—George Mueller

For it is by grace you have been saved, through faith—
and this not from yourselves, it is the gift of God—
not by works, so that no one can boast.

—Ephesians 2:8–9

The Race of Life
Finding a Faithful Pace for the Journey

*Let us fix our eyes on Jesus, the author and perfecter of our faith,
who for the joy set before him endured the cross, scorning its shame,
and sat down at the right hand of the throne of God.*

—Hebrews 12:1–2

You have to wonder about a person who would allow a twelve-foot python snake to roam free in his home. Unfortunately a young man named Grant overlooked the obvious risk, believing that his familiarity with his pet python, Damien, placed him above danger. On October 11, 1996, Grant prepared to feed Damien a chicken, just as he had the week before. Herpetologists suspect that Grant either forgot to wash the smell of the chicken from his hands, or Damien simply desired a larger prey. Whatever the reason, on that fateful day the python decided to wrap himself around Grant.

When a Burmese python is on the brink of a kill, it can move with deadly speed, and rarely can a victim elude its grasp. Grant managed to stagger into the hallway to summon help but soon collapsed in Damien's hold. With great effort the paramedics who arrived were able to uncoil the forty-five-pound, five-inch-thick reptile and hurl it into another room. Grant was rushed to the hospital.

Come to find out, Grant and his brother had been keeping a number of uncaged snakes in their apartment in the Bronx. Their mother had pleaded with them to abandon their hobby, but to no avail. Grant paid dearly for his misplaced faith in Damien the python.[1]

What is faith? According to the writer of Hebrews, faith is "being sure of what we hope for and certain of what we do not see" (Hebrews 11:1). It is a deep conviction—one that is not stagnant or complacent but dynamic in nature. It is an act of believing that overflows from our confidence that something is true or is certain to take place. Going beyond what we can see or touch or feel, we place our faith in something or someone who is worthy of trust.

Grant's problem was that he placed his faith in an unreliable source. Proverbs 13:16 reminds us, "Every prudent man acts out of knowledge, but a fool exposes his folly." Grant's actions were not based on wisdom or prudence but on foolishness. He thought he could trust his python without considering the snake's nature. A python may seem docile at times, but it is—and always will be—a predator that seeks, squeezes, and consumes in order to survive.

Unlike Grant, we must place our faith in a reliable source. But how do we know if something or someone is worthy of our trust? We consider the character (something Grant failed to do when it came to his python). I put my weight on the chair in which I am currently sitting because I have confidence it will hold me up. It is strong and sturdy, it has always held me up before, and I'm sure it won't let me down today. (My computer is another story.) When it comes to sharing my deepest, darkest secrets, I don't spill them to a known gossip but to a loyal friend—someone who has shown herself trustworthy time and time again. I can confidently place my faith in her because her character is proven.

The way we view our world and live our lives is definitely colored by our faith. Do we put our trust in our own abilities and talents? Do we place our confidence in circumstances or fate? Is our hope solely in the goodness of our fellow man? Or do we place our faith in a loving heavenly Father?

The object of our faith is important because that's what floods our lives with purpose. For me, I began to recognize a purpose in my life when I decided to place my faith in Christ. I also began to experience a deep inner peace that only comes from faith in the one true Reliable Source. You may have heard the expression "faith in Christ" before, but do you understand its implications? When we place our faith in Christ, we find both peace and purpose. Let's take a closer look at these two by-products of faith in Jesus.

Peace. "We have peace with God through our Lord Jesus Christ," we read in Romans 5:1. At an early age I learned that God is a perfect and holy God. Man, on the other hand, is sinful and imperfect (no one needed to tell me that part!). Although I was what most people would term a "good little girl," I realized back then that I couldn't earn my way to heaven. The Bible never promises that we get to go through those Pearly Gates if our good deeds outweigh our bad ones. I knew I would never be good enough—but someone else was: Jesus. He was God's perfect gift to mankind. Jesus laid down his life for us as a sacrifice so that, through faith in him, we can have peace with our God.

I will never forget that "aha" moment as a young girl when I first understood that Jesus was more than a baby whose birth we celebrated at Christmas; he was and is the Savior of mankind. At an early age I decided to place my faith in him, praying a prayer something like this:

Dear Lord, thank you for having mercy on me. I know I am not perfect. I know I can't earn my way to heaven. Thank you for sending your Son, Jesus, to die on the cross as a sacrifice for my sin. I place my faith in him as my Savior. I believe he rose from the dead

Expect great things from God. Attempt great things for God. —William Carey

to give us the hope of eternal life in heaven one day. Thank you, Lord, for your grace toward me through Jesus. In his name I pray, amen.

My prayer was simple but based on faith in a God who loves me and wants to have a relationship with me. No big lightning bolts came out of heaven that day, but I knew I had taken an important step. It was the beginning of a life of faith based on the only reliable source in this universe, God himself. Jesus came to bring peace between God and man, and because I was placing my faith in Christ, that peace was now mine.

Purpose. From that day forward I began to recognize a greater purpose in my life. I wasn't just living for myself. Life was bigger than my circumstances. Finally I understood that I have a God who loves me, who has a plan for my life. My desire became to honor him in everything I do. I realized I don't have to perform or be perfect; I just need to walk in his grace.

Often Scripture refers to the plan or purpose God has for his people. King David said, "Many, O LORD my God, are the wonders you have done. The things you planned for us no one can recount to you" (Psalm 40:5). I haven't always known God's purpose for me at different stages of my life. He doesn't reveal his intentions all at once. But step by step, as I've walked with him, I've found that he faithfully leads me according to his plan.

He Is Worthy of Our Trust

Perhaps there has been a time in your life when you've questioned, "Can God be trusted?" Maybe you've been discouraged after the tragic death of a loved one or a disappointing layoff at work or an unwanted divorce. Perhaps you feel even now that God has left you alone in the pit of life. Your faith has been shaken.

You are not alone. Even John the Baptist experienced a time of questioning as he sat in a prison cell. (You can read about it in Luke 7:18–28.) Earlier John had been the one to boldly declare about Jesus, "Look, the Lamb of God, who takes away the sin of the world!" (John 1:29). But now he was in prison, and his faith was faltering. He sent his disciples to ask Jesus, "Are you the one who was to come, or should we expect someone else?"

John could only see the immediate. Sitting in prison, he thought, *Surely this cannot be God's perfect plan. Maybe I was wrong. Maybe God has left me.* Like us, John couldn't see the big picture; he could only see the present. He didn't completely understand what God was up to.

Understanding God and his ways are one thing; trusting him in faith is another. We may have times when we are unable to understand God's thoughts or discern his plan, but we can still trust him. As our Creator and our loving heavenly Father, he has an eternal plan in mind. He sees the whole picture that you and I only see in part. First Corinthians 13:12 explains, "In the same way, we can see and understand only a little about God now, as if we were peering at his reflection in a poor mirror; but someday we are going to see him in his completeness, face to face. Now all that I know is hazy and blurred, but then I will see everything clearly, just as clearly as God sees into my heart right now" (TLB).

I remember times as a teenager when I didn't understand or like my parents' decisions. Still I knew that I could trust their parental love. My parents were especially careful about the parties I attended in junior high and high school. I was horrified when they insisted on calling the host parents of each party to make sure there would be proper supervision. They gave me a curfew that usually fell some time before the party was completely over. I didn't get my way, I didn't like it, I didn't even understand it at the time; but I knew deep inside that my parents loved me and that in doing what they did, they were looking out for my best interest. Because I knew their character, I knew they were worthy of my trust.

No Need to Guess about God

Fortunately, God didn't leave it up to guesswork when it comes to knowing his character. The Bible reveals quite a bit about God's nature. We see his omniscience and authority in the Creation. We catch a glimpse of his power in his deliverance of his people from the ruthless grip of Pharaoh in Egypt. God's patience is revealed in his treatment of the Israelites in the wilderness and through Israel's cycles of straying from the Lord and then returning to him. God's protection is evident in the story of Daniel in the lions' den. His abundant love for us is shown in the sending of his only Son, Jesus, to die for us. His omnipotence is revealed in the Resurrection. We see his kind provision for us in the sending of his Holy Spirit to dwell within us.

Then there are the numerous statements in the Bible that identify God's character:

- *He is good.* "Give thanks to the LORD, for he good; his love endures forever" (Psalm 118:1).

- *He is compassionate.* "The LORD is compassionate and gracious, slow to anger, abounding in love" (Psalm 103:8).

- *He is just.* "The LORD works righteousness and justice for all the oppressed" (Psalm 103:6).

- *He is our protector.* "God is our refuge and strength, an ever-present help in trouble" (Psalm 46:1).

- *He is our helper.* "You are my help and my deliverer" (Psalm 70:5).

- *He is eternal.* "For this is what the high and lofty One says—he who lives forever, whose name is holy" (Isaiah 57:15).

- *He is all-powerful.* "Ah, Sovereign LORD, you have made the heavens and the earth by your great power and outstretched arm. Nothing is too hard for you" (Jeremiah 32:17).

- *He is everywhere.* "Where can I go from your Spirit? Where can I flee from your presence? If I go up to the heavens, you are there; if I make my bed in the depths, you are there" (Psalm 139:7–8).

- *He is all-knowing.* "For God is greater than our hearts, and he knows everything" (1 John 3:20).

- *He is faithful.* "For great is his love toward us, and the faithfulness of the LORD endures forever" (Psalm 117:2).

- *He is perfect.* "As for God, his way is perfect; the word of the LORD is flawless" (Psalm 18:30).

Of course, I have only begun to touch on the greatness of God's character! Yet even in this short list of some of God's wondrous qualities, we can begin to get the sense that he alone is worthy of our ultimate trust. He alone is the Alpha and Omega, the beginning and the end. He is the one reliable source in whom we can confidently place our faith.

Life with a Purpose

Ten years ago I wrote a book called *Parties with a Purpose.* It's a fun book filled with ideas for creating themed parties for kids. Most people who see the title understand the "parties" part, of course, but the "purpose" part is not so obvious. Along with each party theme, I include a valuable lesson to give a specific purpose to each celebration. For instance, the "Dalmatian Sensation" party includes a brief puppet show. The show's star, Danny the Dalmatian, explains to the little party-goers that just as each Dalmatian dog has its own unique set of spots, so each person has special and unique qualities. Each of us is made by God as a unique creation. Kids and parents alike seem to enjoy the idea of putting on a party with a purpose!

What about *Life with a Purpose*? Could that be the title of your personal book? Women of faith throughout history have been motivated by their faith in God to honor him with their lives. Even when they faced hardships, their faith gave them the hope and perseverance they needed to pursue the purposes God set before them.

Take, for instance, Amy Carmichael, born in 1867 in Northern Ireland. Amy came to know Jesus Christ at an early age and had a keen sense of social concern. When she was seventeen years old she led a Sunday school class for the poor mill girls in Belfast. Her class grew to about five hundred people.

At age twenty-six Amy became a missionary to Japan but returned to Ireland fifteen months later due to illness. The next year she continued her missionary work, this time in South India. She stayed there for fifty-six years until she passed away at the age of eighty-four. Her main concern in India was for the temple slavery of little girls. As a religious rite, children were being dedicated to temple gods and given over to prostitution. Amy rescued many young people from this practice and in 1925 founded the Dohnavur Fellowship, dedicated to saving children in moral danger, training them to serve others, and spreading God's love to the people of India. About nine hundred endangered girls and boys were sheltered through the Dohnavur program.

In 1931 Amy had a serious fall that broke her leg, twisted her spine, and left her an invalid for the rest of her life. Her bedroom and her study became her world. She called this place "the Room of Peace," and it was from this room that she began writing extensively. Her written work has blessed and inspired countless thousands—including Elisabeth Elliot, another woman of faith. One of Amy's books, *If,* made

Faith is inseparable from expectations. Where there is real faith, there is always expectation. —Catherine Booth

a lasting impact on Elisabeth, who wrote: "It was from the pages of this ...book that I, a teenager, began to understand the great message of the Cross, of what the author called 'Calvary love.'" Elisabeth eventually wrote Amy's biography, *A Chance to Die*.[2]

What was Amy Carmichael's motivation for leaving her native homeland, creating a refuge for young people in India, and writing countless books of insight and inspiration? *Faith*. Faith in a loving God who had a plan and a purpose for her life. The same faith that led Elisabeth Elliot to minister to the Ecuadorian Aucas, the tribe that had slain her missionary husband in the jungle several years earlier. The same faith that led a woman who was small in stature but big in heart—we know her as Mother Teresa—to begin a school for poor children in Calcutta. Her communities of Missionaries of Charity have grown and expanded to spread Christ's love to the sick, needy, and unwanted in over thirty countries.

"All we do—our prayer, our work, our suffering—is for Jesus," Mother Teresa said. "Our life has no other reason or motivation. This is a point many people do not understand. I serve Jesus twenty-four hours a day. Whatever I do is for him. And he gives me the strength."[3]

It was faith that led two Baylor University girls to share Christ's love in predominately Islamic Afghanistan. Heather Mercer and Dayna Curry were aware of the dangers of ministering in a country hostile to Christianity, but they chose to step out in faith and follow what they believed God was calling them to do. It was their faith that gave them strength through the uncertainty of their three months in Taliban captivity in late 2001. It was faith that kept the precious people of Antioch Community Church in Waco, Texas, praying around the clock for the young women's safety and release. It was God's mercy and grace that allowed Heather and Dayna, along with six others, to be set free.

Faith Stands Up When Our World Falls Down

Our faith in God is the anchor that holds us steady through the storms of life. It reminds us that there is an eternal picture and that this life we can see and touch is only temporary. In the introduction to her book *Tramp for the Lord,* Corrie ten Boom quotes a poem by an anonymous author that speaks of solid faith in an unsure world. She introduces the poem by saying, "Faith is like radar which sees through the fog—the reality of things at a distance that the human eye cannot see." Here is the verse:

My life is but a weaving, between my God and me,
I do not choose the colors, He worketh steadily,
Oftimes He weaveth sorrow, and I in foolish pride,
Forget He sees the upper, and I the underside.
Not till the loom is silent, and shuttles cease to fly,
Will God unroll the canvas and explain the reason why.
The dark threads are as needful in the skillful Weaver's hand,
As the threads of gold and silver in the pattern He has planned.[4]

Oh, the beauty and the blessing of trusting in our eternal heavenly Father who knows the beginning and the end! He sees the full picture; we only see this side. When the storms of life rock our boat, our faith in God allows us to rest our full weight in his safe and loving arms.

As we saw the awful events of September 11 unfold, we also saw people reaching out in faith to God. Churches were flooded as men and women, young and old began looking for answers, hope, purpose, and salvation. Jim Cymbala, pastor of the Brooklyn Tabernacle in New York City, found his church overflowing in the days following the terrorist attack on the World Trade Center. More than 670 people came to faith in Christ that next Sunday. Pastor Cymbala says there has never been a moment like this in our nation's history when so many people were looking toward faith in God.[5]

Faith Is Essential

How is it that a prostitute from a pagan town could be listed among the great people of the Bible—and named as an ancestor of Christ to boot? The answer is simple: She was a woman with a firm faith in the one true God. The Book of Joshua tells the story of the Israelite spies who entered the town of Jericho and found a place to stay at the home of Rahab the harlot. (We won't ask questions about why or how the men ended up at Rahab's house.) Rahab promised to hide the spies and help them if they would spare her family in the imminent battle between her people and the Israelites. In making the offer, she revealed her motivation in a great statement of faith:

> We have heard how the LORD dried up the water of the Red Sea for you when you came out of Egypt, and what you did to Sihon and Og, the two kings of the Amorites east of the Jordan, whom you completely destroyed. When we heard of it, our hearts melted and everyone's courage failed because of you, for the LORD your God is God in heaven above and on the earth below. Now then, please swear to me by the LORD that you will show kindness to my family, because I have shown kindness to you. (Joshua 2:10–12)

Rahab had heard the stories of the mighty works of the God of Israel. Without a doubt those stories made her tremble, but they also moved her to faith, giving her the confidence to declare that "the Lord your God is God in heaven above and on the earth below." Her faith led her to put her life at risk in order to conceal the Israelite spies and help them escape the city safely. For her faithfulness the spies gave her a scarlet cord to put in her window. The approaching Israelites would see the cord, and Rahab and her family would be kept safe in the battle.

Does this remind you of another time when people were saved by something scarlet? Perhaps you are thinking of the Passover, when the Israelites were instructed to place the blood of a lamb on their doorposts so that the angel of death would pass over their homes. All who were inside, behind the marked doorposts, were safe, while the firstborn children in all unmarked homes were killed.

Both of these Old Testament instances are pictures of salvation through faith in Christ. Today we, too, are saved by something scarlet: our faith in Jesus, who shed his blood for us to save us from "the wages of sin" (Romans 6:23).

We can find Rahab listed in the great "Hall of Faith" of Hebrews 11—right next to such notable patriarchs as Noah, Abraham, and Moses! Hebrews 11:31 tells us, "By faith the prostitute Rahab, because she welcomed the spies, was not killed with those who were disobedient." Rahab is also identified in the direct lineage of Jesus in Matthew 1:5: "Salmon the father of Boaz, whose mother was Rahab...."

In God's eyes, what Rahab had been and what she had done in the past were not as important as her faith. Her faith changed her life. Rahab believed in the one true God, and as she acted on that faith, it saved her both physically and spiritually. If God can take a prostitute living in enemy territory and elevate her to a great woman of faith, what can he do with our scarred and tattered lives?

The writer of Hebrews addresses the essential nature of faith: "And without faith it is impossible to please God, because anyone who comes to him must believe that he exists and that he rewards those who earnestly seek him" (Hebrews 11:6). What about you? Have you taken a step of faith in God? Do you believe God loves you and sent his Son,

Jesus, to save you? Just as the scarlet cord saved Rahab and the Passover blood saved the Israelites' firstborn, so the blood of Christ saves us. Paul said, "Believe in the Lord Jesus, and you will be saved" (Acts 16:31). It's all about faith.

Persevere in the Journey

During my college years I decided to enter a marathon. (Yes—that's 26.2 miles of running!) In my youthful exuberance, I agreed to train with one of my Baylor friends through a rigorous twelve-week program. On the day of the race, I knew I was facing one of the biggest physical challenges of my life. But I was ready. Casting aside my warm-ups and any other weight that could possibly hinder me, I waited at the starting line along with my friend and thousands of other runners. Adrenaline flowed as the gunshot signaled the start of the race.

My friend and I parted after about the fifth mile, but I was not alone. My parents, my sister, and my boyfriend, Curt (now my husband), were all there on the sidelines to cheer me on. They held up signs throughout the race and even joined the race to run with me during some of the tough parts.

It was at about the twenty-second mile that I "hit the wall." Long distance runners are familiar with this phase. It refers to the physical and mental point you reach when you feel as though you can't go one more step. Some people stop running at this point; others give up completely. But most simply persevere through the wall, knowing that the finish line is not far away.

My goal for this race was to finish. It didn't matter to me how long it took; I just wanted to finish. When I hit the wall, all I could do was picture the finish line. I slowed my pace and even walked for a short while, but I kept the finish line foremost in my mind. I knew I would eventually get there. And when I crossed that line, the joy and the sense of accomplishment were overwhelming. The race took me a little over four hours from start to finish, but it was an epoch in my life. I learned through that experience what it means to set a goal, prepare for it, and follow through to the end.

Life is like a marathon—although many times we live it like a sprint. It is a long journey filled with both joys and difficulties. We are bound to hit the wall many times during this race of life. That's why Paul encourages us to "fix our eyes on Jesus, the author and perfecter of our faith" (Hebrews 12:2).

Where is our focus? Is it on the One who is worthy of our faith? Great women of faith have journeyed down this road before us, keeping their eyes steadfastly on Jesus. They were able to stay the course because they cast off the things that entangled them and ran with diligence to the finish line. Like Rahab, Amy Carmichael, Elisabeth Elliot, and Mother Teresa, may you and I run with perseverance the race of life marked out for us!

POWER POINT

Read: The story of Ruth in Ruth 1:1–5, 15–18, and 4:13–22. What great statement of faith did Ruth make? What steps of faith did Ruth take? How was Ruth's faithfulness rewarded?

Pray: Wonderful heavenly Father, I thank you for the peace and the purpose you give to my life. I put my faith in you because you are worthy. Help me to walk in faith, trusting you for the big picture of life. I may not understand all that you do or allow, but I trust your loving grace to see me through every circumstance. Lead me step by step in faith as I follow you. In Jesus' name I pray, amen.

💡 **Remember:** "For it is by grace you have been saved, through faith—and this not from yourselves, it is the gift of God—not by works, so that no one can boast" (Ephesians 2:8–9).

☺ **Do:** When did you first take a step in faith toward God? Write down your story so you can share it with your family and others. If you have never placed your faith and trust in Christ, perhaps this would be a good time to pray a prayer similar to the one I shared in this chapter.

Spiritual Makeover
Faith in Action: Putting on a Whole New Wardrobe

As the body without the spirit is dead,
so faith without deeds is dead.

—James 2:26

In the early eighties (okay, I'm dating myself), several cosmetic lines began a new sales technique that involved identifying a woman's best color scheme. Color consultants draped an array of colorful swatches across a woman's shoulders in order to determine which colors looked best with her natural skin tone. A woman with blond hair, blue eyes, and fair skin was typically identified as a "summer," meaning she looked her best in colors such as pink, purple, and black. A brunette with an olive complexion was most likely a "fall," implying she looked her best in browns, greens, and oranges. Dark hair and fair skin usually marked a "winter" and called for a different color scheme, while still others looked best in a "spring" palette. I had my colors done several times and consistently turned out to be a "summer."

Since I didn't know I was a "summer" until this testing, I had collected a rainbow array of clothes over the years—and not just pinks and purples. Now all the brown, green, yellow, and orange garments in my closet needed to go. I couldn't walk around in "fall" colors if I was a "summer." What a fashion faux pas! From that point on, I determined, I wouldn't be caught dead in brown. Of course, I had to pitch my old makeup colors too. No more blushes with an orange tint; it was pink all the way for me, baby!

We often make changes in our lives according to our beliefs. Some changes are bigger than others. My color makeover was based on my newfound conviction that I was a "summer." The more I learned about seasonal color schemes, the more my wardrobe began to reflect "summer" colors.

When we put our faith in Christ, our lives go through another type of makeover—a *spiritual* makeover. As we become women of faith, our behavior begins to change to reflect our newfound beliefs. Of course, our actions and behavior are not what save us in God's eyes; we are saved by his grace through faith alone (see Ephesians 2:8–9). Our works do not lead to salvation; if they did, we would have reason to be boastful. It is our faith that pleases the Lord (see Hebrews 11:6).

Still, our actions *are* important. Why? Because they are an evidence of our faith.

A Living Example

In the New Testament, James speaks heartily about the connection between faith and works: "What good is it, my brothers, if a man claims to have faith but has no deeds? Can such faith save him? Suppose a brother or sister is without clothes or daily food. If one of you says to him, 'Go, I wish you well; keep warm and well fed,' but does nothing about his physical needs, what good is it? In the same way, faith by itself, if it is not accompanied by action, is dead" (James 2:14–17).

Let's be clear. James is not saying that we please God or make it to heaven by doing good deeds. He is saying that if we have a living faith in Christ, it should be evident in our actions. The "new us" should be reflected in our behavior.

We may be able to quote all the right Bible verses and talk as if we have great faith, but unless that faith is played out in our lives, we have very little evidence that it is real. These are tough words. But as positive women of faith, it is important that we be consistent in what we say and do. My dad has often quoted a poem attributed to Edgar Guest, which speaks to the power of our actions. It's called "Sermons We See":

I'd rather see a sermon than hear one any day.

I'd rather one would walk with me—than merely show the way.

The eye's a better pupil—more willing than the ear,

Fine counsel is confusing, but examples always clear.

And the best of all the people are the ones who live their creed,

For to see the good in action is what everybody needs,

I can soon learn how to do it if you'll let me see it done,

I can watch your hands in action, but your tongue too fast may run.

The lectures you deliver may be very wise and true—

But I'd rather get my lesson by observing what you do.

For I may misunderstand you, and the high advice you give,

But there's no misunderstanding how you act and how you live.[1]

Bible scholars have wrestled for centuries over the proper understanding of faith's relationship to works. C. S. Lewis described this tension when he wrote, "The controversy about faith and works is one that has gone on for a very long time, and it is a highly technical matter. I personally rely on the paradoxical text: 'Work out your own salvation...for it is God that worketh in you.' It looks as if in one sense we do nothing, and in another case we do a...lot. 'Work out your own salvation with fear and trembling,' but you must have it in you before you can work it out."[2]

Certainly we must balance the beauty and wonder of God's grace with the powerful evidence of his grace at work in us. The works we see in our lives are not a result of our own power; they are evidence of God's Spirit working in us. God freely gives us salvation. Will he not also freely give us to the power to live it out?

I love the illustration Jim Cymbala, pastor of the Brooklyn Tabernacle in New York City, provides in his book, *Fresh Power:* "Imagine that my sister, Pat, and her husband, Frank, come over to my house for Christmas, bringing a lovely present for Carol and me. Pat greets me at the front door with a warm hug. 'Here, this is for you!' she exclaims as she hands me a large box wrapped in metallic paper and a fancy bow. 'Merry Christmas! By the way, that'll be $55, please—cash or check. Either one is fine, but I don't take credit cards.'"[3]

It is preposterous to think that someone would give us a gift and then ask us to pay for it. Well, I guess my teenagers do that sometimes. But not God! God freely gives us the gift of his Spirit to work mightily in our lives. The Holy Spirit is God's makeup artist, sent to give us a spiritual makeover—at no charge to us. Ephesians 4:30 says, "And do not grieve the Holy Spirit of God, with whom you were sealed for the day of redemption." May we never be guilty of hindering the Spirit's work!

Cleaning Out the Closet

To say that I revamped my entire wardrobe just because I found out I was a "summer" sounds silly, I know. What can I tell you? I fell victim to a trendy marketing scheme. But not all overhauls are so shallow and short-lived. For example, when I placed my faith in Christ, I had a spiritual makeover of the eternal type. You could say I became a new creation—at least that's how the apostle Paul describes it in 2 Corinthians 5:17: "Therefore, if anyone is in Christ, he is a new creation; the old has gone, the new has come!" How refreshing to begin anew, to start walking in faith, to allow God to change me from the inside out!

What does this "new creation" look like? We find descriptions of our new wardrobe throughout the Bible. In Colossians 3:1–15, Paul talks about cleaning out our closets, so to speak, and putting on new clothes. Let's take a look at his makeover advice:

> Since, then, you have been raised with Christ, set your hearts on things above, where Christ is seated at the right hand of God. Set your minds on things above, not on earthly things. For you died, and your life is now hidden with Christ in God. When Christ, who is your life, appears, then you also will appear with him in glory.
>
> Put to death, therefore, whatever belongs to your earthly nature: sexual immorality, impurity, lust, evil desires and greed, which is idolatry. Because of these, the wrath of God is coming. You used to walk in these ways, in the life you once lived. But now you must rid yourselves of all such things as these: anger, rage, malice, slander, and filthy language from your lips. Do not lie to each other, since you have taken off your old self with its practices and have put on the new self, which is being renewed in knowledge in the image of its Creator....
>
> Therefore, as God's chosen people, holy and dearly loved, clothe yourselves with compassion, kindness, humility, gentleness and patience. Bear with each other and forgive whatever grievances you may have against one another. Forgive as the Lord forgave you. And over all these virtues put on love, which binds them all together in perfect unity.
>
> Let the peace of Christ rule in your hearts, since as members of one body you were called to peace. And be thankful.

Paul covers it all, from our hearts to our minds to our actions. Living a life based on faith in Christ ought to look different than a life lived for self and the here-and-now. This overhaul is a work of God's

If faith produces no works, I see that faith is not a living tree. Thus faith and works together grow; no separate life they e'er can know; they're soul and body, hand and heart; what God hath joined, let no man part. —Hannah More

☺

Spirit, not of our flesh. God, who began this good work in us, has promised he will carry it on to completion (see Philippians 1:6). His Spirit empowers us to live a life of love and forgiveness, and by his Spirit we are able to bear with one another and abide in unity.

Unfortunately, we see very few Christians today who are clothed in these outward signs of an inward faith. Has God's wellspring of power gone dry in our lives? Or are we failing to allow his Spirit to live mightily through us?

Wouldn't It Be Lovely?

If we truly lived in the new clothes Paul describes, wouldn't we be lovely? More than that, wouldn't people be drawn to Christ because we were living such beautiful lives of faith? Could there be a lovelier, more positive woman of faith than one who is clothed with compassion, kindness, humility, gentleness, and patience? Who bears with others and forgives them? Who exudes love and peace? A woman wearing such an outfit would be asked continually where she did her shopping, and the answer would be, "At the feet of Jesus."

Unfortunately, the world rarely sees this type of fashion show when they look at Christians and the church. Instead they see gossip and bickering, disloyalty and bitterness, jealousy and envy. Not very attractive, would you say? Oh friend in faith, if only the new look could start with you and me! Perhaps we could begin to model Christ's love to others and make a real difference in this world. The fruit of God's Spirit in our lives is beautiful. Listen to the description in Galatians 5:19–25:

> The acts of the sinful nature are obvious: sexual immorality, impurity and debauchery; idolatry and witchcraft; hatred, discord, jealousy, fits of rage, selfish ambition, dissensions, factions and envy;

drunkenness, orgies, and the like. I warn you, as I did before, that those who live like this will not inherit the kingdom of God.

But the fruit of the Spirit is love, joy, peace, patience, kindness, goodness, faithfulness, gentleness and self-control. Against such things there is no law. Those who belong to Christ Jesus have crucified the sinful nature with its passions and desires. Since we live by the Spirit, let us keep in step with the Spirit.

As positive women, may we clothe ourselves with the lovely garments of the fruit of the Spirit. May we allow God's Spirit to pour through us and touch this world with Christ's love.

Faith Accessories

Here's a phrase we hear women say quite often: "Oh, I'm just a worrier." We all seem to have anxieties in different areas of life. My mother used to worry about the house always looking clean and perfect. I, on the other hand, worry about the safety of my kids. One of my friends worries about the future. Another friend who is in sales worries about commissions. What do *you* worry about? Worry is an all-too-common thread among women, and we have grown accustomed to it in our lives. But should we?

If faith is truly at work, it leaves little room for worry or fear. An inscription at Hind's Head Inn in Bray, England, says, "Fear knocked at the door. Faith answered. No one was there."[4] Isn't that tremendous? When faith meets fear, worry and doubt disappear. According to George MacDonald, "A perfect faith would lift us absolutely above fear."[5]

How do we grow in our faith to the point that we don't worry? Oddly enough, we can glean our answer from a man in prison. The

Faith does nothing alone—nothing of itself, but everything under God, by God, through God. —William Stoughton

apostle Paul wrote to the Philippians, "Do not be anxious about anything, but in everything, by prayer and petition, with thanksgiving, present your requests to God. And the peace of God, which transcends all understanding, will guard your hearts and your minds in Christ Jesus" (Philippians 4:6–7). When worry and fear seem to be getting the best of you, pray! Turn your cares over to God through faith in prayer. This is a daily activity, for worries frequently seem to come back and attack us. But Paul tells us we can experience a peace that passes all understanding if we will place our worries in God's hands.

George Mueller was a man of faith. As the founder of numerous orphanages in nineteenth-century England, he depended entirely on God for food and supplies for the orphans under his care. He never asked for a dime in donations but rather, through faith, prayed about every need. God richly blessed Mueller's life of faith, and the orphans never went without. Concerning anxiety, Mueller said, "The beginning of anxiety is the end of faith, and the beginning of true faith is the end of anxiety."[6]

What would our lives look like if they were characterized by less worry and more faith? If we truly trusted God for our future, for our strength, for our direction? If we moved forward in faith instead of worrying about how to make something happen ourselves? Just think about the impact our lives would have if we were to prayerfully live a life of faith day by day. We may never be famous or have an opportunity to influence thousands of people, but if we each walk in faith right where God has placed us, together we can make a positive difference in this world.

Stepping Out in Faith

Faith is stepping forward as God directs, even when we don't know what the outcome will be. It's doing something bigger than ourselves—so big that we are dependent on God and not on our own strength and ability. When we step out in faith, God gets the glory, because whatever is accomplished is done by his Spirit at work through us. We can read a roster of heroes and heroines of the faith in Hebrews 11. God accomplished great things through each of these people as they simply stepped out in faith. Take a look at the lineup:

- Verse 7: "By faith Noah, when warned about things not yet seen, in holy fear built an ark to save his family."

- Verse 8: "By faith Abraham, when called to go to a place he would later receive as his inheritance, obeyed and went, even though he did not know where he was going."

- Verse 9: "By faith he made his home in the promised land like a stranger in a foreign country."

- Verse 11: "By faith Abraham, even though he was past age—and Sarah herself was barren—was enabled to become a father because he considered him faithful who had made the promise."

- Verse 17: "By faith Abraham, when God tested him, offered Isaac as a sacrifice."

- Verse 20: "By faith Isaac blessed Jacob and Esau in regard to their future."

- Verse 21: "By faith Jacob, when he was dying, blessed each of Joseph's sons, and worshiped as he leaned on the top of his staff."

- Verse 22: "By faith Joseph, when his end was near, spoke about the exodus of the Israelites from Egypt and gave instructions about his bones."

- Verse 23: "By faith Moses' parents hid him for three months after he was born, because they saw he was no ordinary child, and they were not afraid of the king's edict."

- Verses 24–28: "By faith Moses, when he had grown up, refused to be known as the son of Pharaoh's daughter....By faith he left Egypt, not fearing the king's anger; he persevered because he saw him who is invisible. By faith he kept the Passover and the sprinkling of blood, so that the destroyer of the firstborn would not touch the firstborn of Israel."

- Verse 29: "By faith the people passed through the Red Sea as on dry land."

- Verse 30: "By faith the walls of Jericho fell, after the people had marched around them for seven days."

- Verse 31: "By faith the prostitute Rahab, because she welcomed the spies, was not killed with those who were disobedient."

- Verses 32–35: "What more shall I say? I do not have time to tell about Gideon, Barak, Samson, Jephthah, David, Samuel and the prophets who through faith conquered kingdoms, administered justice, and gained what was promised; who shut the mouths of lions, quenched the fury of the flames, and escaped the edge of the sword; whose weakness was turned to strength; and who became powerful in battle and routed foreign armies. Women received back their dead, raised to life again."

Wow! Do you feel like you have just been on a roller coaster ride through the Old Testament with a park full of faithful followers? Despite all the ups and downs, each person on this ride stayed on the track of faith. Each one received a heavenly blessing—and sometimes an earthly one too.

As each one found out, stepping out in faith is no guarantee of a perfectly smooth ride in this life. In fact, some of the people who stepped out in faith were tortured, jeered, and flogged; others were chained, imprisoned, and stoned (see Hebrews 11:35–39). Clearly, a life of faith is not a life without challenges. But it is a life of victory nonetheless. The writer of Hebrews says of these faithful followers, "the world was not worthy of them" (v. 38). God's plan is bigger than the immediate; it is bigger than what we see or experience in the here and now. Who knows what great work he can and will do with our simple step of faith?

The faithful steps of these Old Testament men and women paved the way for our lives of faith today. Hebrews 11 closes with this statement: "These were all commended for their faith, yet none of them received what had been promised. God had planned something better for us so that only together with us would they be made perfect" (vv. 39–40). We may never see the full blessing of our step of faith until heaven. May we be faithful to hear his call in our lives and take the steps he directs us to take, leaving the results to him. A. W. Pink puts it this way: "Faith is a principle of life by which the Christian lives unto God; a principle of motion, by which he walks to heaven along the highway of holiness; a principle of strength, by which he opposes the flesh, the world, and the devil."[7]

A Modern-Day Woman of Faith

What can happen if we hear God's call and step out in faith? Mary Kay Ash, founder of the Mary Kay Cosmetics company, is a modern-day example of a woman of faith. Her life message was simple: God first, family second, career third. At her funeral, Reverend C. Robert Hasley said, "Mary Kay Ash was one of God's most faithful messengers. She was a saint."[8] Carolyn Dickinson, director of sales development for Mary Kay, Inc., told me this about the company and its founder:

It all began thirty-eight years ago with a dream for all women to fulfill themselves to be what God intended them to be. She stepped up to the plate and made the choice to do what he was telling her to do. Back in the early sixties, a time of injustice for women in the workplace, Mary Kay made the courageous decision to invest her entire life savings of five thousand dollars to follow God's will and change the world through compassion and hope, a lesson from which we can all learn.

Carolyn also told me about a time in 1979 when Mary Kay was interviewed on the popular television show *Sixty Minutes*. She was asked, "Mary Kay, you talk about God being your first priority. Aren't you using God to further your business?" She responded with the perfect answer: "I surely hope not. I hope he is using me." And he certainly did. At the time of her death in November 2001, Mary Kay, Inc., reported revenue of $1.3 billion. But more importantly, through her company, thousands of women's lives had been touched and changed.

Mary Kay once said, "Most people live and die with their music still unplayed. They never dare to try."[9] Certainly Mary Kay Ash dared to step out in faith. She not only acted on her faith in God, she showed her faith in people as well. She encouraged her sales force with the confidence they needed to succeed.

"She taught us well," said Mary Kay's son, Richard Rogers. "Those of us that know her and love her have benefited in our lives from her teachings. Her belief in the beautiful potential inside every human being was a cornerstone, and this became the cornerstone of everyone she touched."[10]

It has been said that Mary Kay Ash gave the women of this world a makeover, offering them the opportunity to join the working world from their own homes. I believe she also offers us a model of a woman who allowed God to give her a spiritual makeover. Her love, kindness, and inspiration—led by God's direction and done in his power—show us what a woman of faith looks like when she puts on her new wardrobe. Her life reminds us to never underestimate what God can do through a willing heart and a step of faith.

Of course, most of the positive women of faith in the world today are women we have never heard of. They are sweet, humble women who walk a life of faith step by step, day by day. They may never achieve fame, but they *are* making a positive difference in the lives of the people around them. They are the faithful prayer warriors at church, the faithful mothers encouraging their children, the faithful employees working heartily as unto the Lord. Whether the results they achieve are big or small, their reward in heaven is profound. And each one can look forward to the day when they are greeted with these words: "Well done, thou good and faithful servant."

POWER POINT

⚙ **Read:** Exodus 1:6 to 2:10, the stories of three women who acted in faith. How did the two Hebrew midwives show their faith in God? In what way did the Levite woman, who is later identified in Scripture as Jochebed (Exodus 6:20), show her faith? What was the result of her faithful actions?

♡ **Pray:** O Giver of Life, thank you for working in my life! Thank you for changing me and making me a new creation in you. In every area of my life, help me to reflect your Spirit living inside of me. I want to honor and glorify you in all I do and say. May my faith be evident as a result of your work in me. In the name of my faithful Savior, Jesus, amen.

💡 **Remember:** "And without faith it is impossible to please God, because anyone who comes to him must believe that he exists and that he rewards those who earnestly seek him" (Hebrews 11:6).

☺ **Do:** Take time to listen to God. Is he telling you to step out in faith in a certain direction? Are you holding back because of fear, anxiety, or lack of self-confidence? Remember, where we are weak, he is strong. Allow God to direct your paths, step out in faith, and watch him work through you.

Power Principle #2

Becoming A Woman OF Wisdom

Knowledge comes, but wisdom lingers.

—Alfred, Lord Tennyson

For the LORD gives wisdom, and
from his mouth come knowledge and understanding....
For wisdom will enter your heart,
and knowledge will be pleasant to your soul.

—Proverbs 2:6, 10

More Precious Than Rubies
Searching for Wisdom in All the Right Places

It is better to get wisdom than gold.
Gold is another's, wisdom is our own;
gold is for the body and time, wisdom for the soul and eternity.

—Matthew Henry

Wit and wisdom can be found in the oddest places. Bumper stickers, refrigerator magnets, T-shirts, greeting cards, and even decorative pillows tout some of life's best quips. Here are some of my favorites:

- A waist is a terrible thing to mind.

- Anything free is worth what you pay for it.

- Atheism is a nonprophet organization.

- I used to be indecisive; now I'm not so sure.

- My reality check just bounced.

- Everyone is entitled to my opinion.

- It's all about *you,* isn't it?

- Help stamp out and eradicate superfluous redundancy.

- What if there were no hypothetical questions?

- At my age, I've seen it all, done it all, heard it all...I just can't remember it all.

- If I had known being a grandmother was so much fun, I would have done it first!

- *Veni, Vidi, Visa:* I came, I saw, I did a little shopping.

- What if the Hokey Pokey is really what it's all about?

It's fun to discover little gems of wisdom in unexpected places. I'm sure you've discovered a few of your own favorites. I especially liked one T-shirt I saw that pointed to the ultimate source of wisdom. It had a picture of an open Bible and the caption "When all else fails, read the directions." Sometimes reading the directions is our last resort when we're playing a board game or putting together a dollhouse. But when it comes to getting direction in life, we neglect reading our Maker's instructions to our own peril!

As positive women, our search for wisdom ought to take us far beyond gift shop paraphernalia. Certainly T-shirts, bumper stickers, and magnets can offer some fun and frivolous perspectives on life; but when it comes to wisdom, we must pursue a solid base of truth.

Wisdom Defined

Wisdom is a common word used and treasured throughout the ages. But what does it mean to be a woman of wisdom? Webster defines wisdom as "sagacity, discernment or insight." It also calls wisdom "scholarly knowledge or learning." *The New Open Bible* defines wisdom as "knowledge guided by understanding." Putting it all together, we can say that wisdom is a type of application of the knowledge we possess. It is not knowledge in and of itself. I like what Frank M. Garafda says: "The difference between a smart man and a wise man is that a smart man knows what to say, and a wise man knows whether to say it or not."[1]

Solomon, the ancient king of Israel who is widely accepted as one of the wisest people the world has ever known, said, "The fear of the LORD is the beginning of wisdom, and knowledge of the Holy One is understanding" (Proverbs 9:10). In other words, "Do you want wisdom? Then here is the starting point: Fear God."

Stop reading for a moment and ponder the phrase "the fear of the Lord." What does it mean? According to Matthew Henry's commentary, this "fear" is "a reverence of God's majesty and a dread of his wrath." A reverence and awe of God, both in heart and in mind, is where we must begin the process of seeking to be wise. It's the ground floor in the tower of wisdom.

We can see this played out in many ways through life. Our fear of God keeps us from making foolish choices. Take Allison, for example. She is almost guaranteed a big promotion if she simply fudges on some numbers that represent sales quotas for the last quarter. Most likely no one would check the actual accounting. She has been hoping to redecorate her house, and the promotion would give her the income to do it. But Allison fears God and knows that those who seek dishonest gain come to ruin. Even if no one found out about it, God would know. She makes the wise decision to keep the numbers honest.

Wisdom has to do with both lifestyle and discernment. Proverbs 8:13 explains, "To fear the LORD is to hate evil; I [wisdom] hate pride and arrogance, evil behavior and perverse speech." Every day we have choices that confront us. Some are big and some are small, but all of our choices demand wisdom. On what will we base our decisions? A wise person makes decisions based on the understanding that God and his time-honored principles are the only sure foundation for life. A foolish person does not act on the foundation of a reverence for God and instead lives recklessly for selfish gain.

I think about the parable of the wise man who built his house upon a rock. When the rains came down and the floods came up, the house

The greatest good is wisdom. —St. Augustine

on the rock stood firm. Meanwhile the foolish man built his house on the sand; when the rains came down and the floods came up, the house on the sand fell. (You can read this parable in Luke 6:46–49.) Jesus told this story to say that if we come to him, hear his words, and do what he says, our lives will be lived on a sure foundation. If we don't—if we fail to respect and honor God's principles—our lives will be shaky and unstable. Leo Tolstoy put it this way: "Each will have to make his own choice: to oppose the will of God, building upon the sands the unstable house of his brief, illusive life, or to join in the eternal, deathless movement of true life in accordance with God's will."[2]

The House of Wisdom

Everyone is invited to dwell in the magnificent house of wisdom. The invitation is found in Proverbs 9:1–10:

Wisdom has built her house; she has hewn out its seven pillars. She has prepared her meat and mixed her wine; she has also set her table. She has sent out her maids, and she calls from the highest point of the city. "Let all who are simple come in here!" she says to those who lack judgment. "Come, eat my food and drink the wine I have mixed. Leave your simple ways and you will live; walk in the way of understanding.…Instruct a wise man and he will be wiser still; teach a righteous man and he will add to his learning. The fear of the LORD is the beginning of wisdom, and knowledge of the Holy One is understanding."

Don't you just love the fact that wisdom is presented in the feminine form in Proverbs? I gladly pointed out that fact to my husband! Lest we become puffed up with pride too quickly, however, it is important to note that *folly* is also presented as a woman in this chapter, and she has an invitation of her own: "The woman Folly is loud; she is undisciplined and without knowledge. She sits at the door of her house, on a seat at the highest point of the city, calling out to those who pass by, who go straight on their way. 'Let all who are simple come in here!' she says to those who lack judgment" (Proverbs 9:13–16).

Two invitations await each of us. Which one will we accept? Wherever we are, whatever our situation, we can choose to go to wisdom's banquet and be a no-show at the other. If we move one step at a time in the right direction, with the fear of the Lord as our foundation, we soon will find ourselves at wisdom's open door. As Benjamin Franklin said, "The Doors of Wisdom are never shut."[3]

The Proper Outfit

Like all banquets, wisdom's banquet requires appropriate attire. Before we visit the house of wisdom, we must first cast off our simple ways and walk in the way of understanding, as Proverbs 9:6 says. In fact, a quick search through the Book of Proverbs identifies a number of the qualities with which we should adorn ourselves:

- *Righteousness.* "Instruct a wise man and he will be wiser still; teach a righteous man and he will add to his learning" (Proverbs 9:9).

- *An obedient heart and quiet tongue.* "The wise in heart accept commands, but a chattering fool comes to ruin" (Proverbs 10:8).

- *A listening ear.* "Now then, my sons, listen to me; blessed are those who keep my ways. Listen to my instruction and be wise; do not ignore it. Blessed is the man who listens to me, watching daily at my doors, waiting at my doorway" (Proverbs 8:32–34).

- *Discernment.* "Wisdom is found on the lips of the discerning" (Proverbs 10:13). "Let the wise listen and add to their learning, and let the discerning get guidance" (Proverbs 1:5).

We need to be properly dressed because, at wisdom's party, we will undoubtedly find ourselves rubbing shoulders with the other guests. Proverbs 8:12 and 8:14 introduce us to a few of wisdom's closest friends. No banquet would be complete without them: "I, wisdom, dwell together with prudence; I possess knowledge and discretion.... Counsel and sound judgment are mine; I have understanding and power."

Prudence. Knowledge. Discretion. Counsel. Sound judgment. Understanding. Power. We find each of these whenever we pursue godly wisdom. In his classic work, *Leviathan,* Thomas Hobbes said, "Knowledge is power." But a truer saying is "Wisdom is power." Wisdom is a great deal more than intellectual awareness. It involves knowledge, yes, but also discretion, sound judgment, and all the rest. Most importantly, wisdom includes a healthy fear of the Lord. When we find wisdom, we become positive women capable of having a powerful impact on our world.

Looking in All the Right Places

Is wisdom an exclusive and snobbish party hostess, or is she kind and available to greet her guests? Lucille Ball once said, "In life, all good things come hard, but wisdom is the hardest to come by."[4] I have to say, Lucy is partly right; wisdom *is* hard to find—unless you know where to look. Proverbs 8:17 says, "I [wisdom] love those who love me, and those who seek me find me." Wisdom is waiting for us to find her. We simply need to look in the right places. Where do we begin?

God's Word. The Bible contains the actual words of our omniscient Creator and loving heavenly Father, making it the perfect starting point. Why in the world would we ignore it? People throughout the ages have looked to the Bible for wisdom. The famous Italian astronomer Galileo once said, "I am inclined to think that the authority of Holy Scripture is intended to convince men of those truths which are necessary for their salvation, which, being far above man's understanding, cannot be made credible by any learning, or any other means than revelation by the Holy Spirit."[5]

Abraham Lincoln was another great man who valued the wisdom of God's Word. He had this to say upon receiving a Bible as a gift: "In regard to this Great Book, I have but to say, I believe the Bible is the best gift God has given to man. All the good Savior gave to the world was communicated through this Book. But for this Book we could not know right from wrong. All things most desirable for man's welfare, here and hereafter, are to be found portrayed in it."[6]

Scripture itself confirms the powerful and credible wisdom found within its pages. The apostle Peter writes, "We have the prophetic word confirmed, which you do well to heed as a light that shines in a dark place....Knowing this first, that no prophecy of Scripture is of any private interpretation, for prophecy never came by the will of man, but holy men of God spoke as they were moved by the Holy Spirit" (2 Peter 1:19–21 NKJV). Timothy says that all Scripture is "God-breathed" (2 Timothy 3:16). That makes the Bible wisdom's most reliable source.

Prayer. James tells us, "If any of you lacks wisdom, he should ask God, who gives generously to all without finding fault, and it will be given to him" (James 1:5). When was the last time you prayed for God to grant you wisdom? According to the Bible, all we have to do is ask, and he will freely give it to us.

I'm reminded of the wonderful request Solomon made of God. In 1 Kings 3:5, God said to Solomon, "Ask for whatever you want me to give you." Solomon could have asked for wealth or fame or honor or even happiness. Instead he asked for a wise and discerning heart to guide his people. God was so pleased with Solomon's request—which he of course fulfilled—that he also granted him riches and honor. Can you imagine the smile that would light a mother's face if her child said to her, "Mom, you are so wise. Can you help me think through this important decision?" I think God smiles like that when we ask for wisdom and discernment to help us along life's way.

Our nation's first president, George Washington, knew the value of seeking God's wisdom and protection on a daily basis. On May 1, 1777, as news finally came that France would be assisting the American troops in the Revolutionary War, he prayed, "And now, Almighty Father, if it is Thy holy will that we shall obtain a place and name among the nations of the earth, grant that we may be enabled to show our gratitude for Thy goodness by our endeavors to fear and obey Thee. Bless us with Thy wisdom in our counsels, success in battle, and let all our victories be tempered with humanity."[7] Obviously Washington was a man of great faith and a great example to us. He knew where to turn for wisdom and strength.

Jeremiah 33:2–3 says, "This is what the LORD says, he who made the earth, the LORD who formed it and established it—the LORD is his name: 'Call to me and I will answer you and tell you great and unsearchable things you do not know.'" Now that's an offer we can't refuse. The God of all creation wants to show us great and mighty things! It almost makes me think of Ed McMahon standing at my door with a million-dollar check from the Publisher's Clearinghouse sweepstakes. There he is, holding out a highly valuable gift in earthly terms, and all I need to do is open the door! God says that all we need to do is call on him, and he will grant us one of the greatest treasures on earth: wisdom.

Wisdom on Tap

Have you seen the new backpack water supply designed for long-distance runners and bikers? It's a half-gallon jug of water that can be strapped to the athlete's back. A long straw runs along the strap, ending

Wisdom is supreme; therefore get wisdom. Though it cost all you have, get understanding. Esteem her, and she will exalt you; embrace her and she will honor you. —Proverbs 4:7–8

near the mouth. It is actually a brilliant invention and a handy way for runners and bikers to have the water resource they need at their disposal. I remember taking long-distance runs with my friends at Baylor University while we were training for a marathon. During the course of a ten-mile run, we needed to drink water. But since we didn't want to carry an extra load in our hands, we depended on local fast food establishments to supply us with a cup of water. We had to break stride to fill up, but water was essential. I think the water backpack is the perfect solution for athletes who want to complete their journeys without interruption.

Did you know there is a kind of "spiritual backpack" we can wear to refresh us along the journey of life? It's called memorizing God's Word. King David said, "I have thought much about your words, and stored them in my heart so that they would hold me back from sin....Nothing is perfect except your words. Oh, how I love them. I think about them all day long. They make me wiser than my enemies, because they are my constant guide" (Psalm 119:11, 96–98 TLB). In my own life, I have found that memorizing Scripture has provided a vital mental resource to help me through difficult times. You have already noticed the memory verses I've included for you in the Power Point sections of each chapter. Let me give you some hints and ideas to help you memorize these verses and others.

Write it. As a former schoolteacher, I know the value of involving as many of the five senses as possible in order to seal ideas, words, and facts in our minds. Once you choose a Scripture verse to place in your heart, write it out several times to begin the sealing process. I suggest using three-by-five index cards. Take the time to write the verse neatly and clearly. Make it easy to read. Write the same verse on three separate cards, and don't forget to include the reference. Say the verse aloud as you write.

Many times I will write a scripture in a creative way to help me identify key words and remember the verse in phrases. Here's an example using Jeremiah 33:3:

Call *to me*
and I will **answer** *you and*
Tell you **great** *and* **unsearchable** *things*
you do not know.

You may want to consider using a variety of colors to help you remember key words. The better you can "see" the verse visually in your mind, the easier it will be to remember it. Sometimes I substitute numbers for the words "for" and "to." I also draw pictures to help me memorize. Sometimes silly pictures are the best! I know it sounds funny, but when I memorize a verse that begins with the words "let us," I draw a head of lettuce to help me remember. Our brains tend to remember pictures (especially silly ones) better than they remember words on a page.

See it. Some time ago I purchased three small plastic frames for one dollar apiece at a local craft store. That was easy! Now when I write out a verse, I place the handwritten cards in the frames and set them around the house in places where I am sure to see them. I keep one frame by my kitchen sink, one in the laundry room, and one on my bathroom counter where I do my makeup.

Why not try it? You can have fun decorating the frames with stickers or small objects to add flare and help catch your attention. You can also buy a frame with a magnet on the back for your refrigerator and a smaller-sized frame for your key chain to carry with you in the car. The more you see the verse, the more you will be reminded to practice saying it.

Speak it. Say your verse aloud at least once a day, perhaps just before you brush your teeth in the morning. My husband always repeats his verse before he turns on the radio in his car. When you speak it and hear it, you help to seal it more deeply in your mind. Try to find one opportunity each week to say the verse to someone else, whether in casual conversation or as an exercise with your family at the dinner table or in the car.

Review it. Typically, Sunday is a day of rest from the normal routine and often a day of spiritual reflection. I recommend using this day to choose a new verse, write it on three new index cards, and change out the frames. Place one of the old cards in a "review box." This can be a cute recipe box or decorated file box. (I am a visual person, so everything I do has to be decorated and cute!) Review the verses in your box once a month—perhaps on the first Sunday—as a refresher. Then every January 1, clean out the box, review each card, put a rubber band around the stack, and store it. Yes, I'm talking about memorizing fifty-two Bible verses a year. But with God's help, you can do it!

If you need more motivation, consider this. According to research, brain cells die as we get older. (I didn't really need a scientist to tell me that.) But recent studies show that fewer cells die when the brain is stimulated with new information. So there you have it—memorizing scripture can help keep our minds young and fresh. What a great additional benefit!

The Wisdom of Friends

Amy and Leslie are heart-friends to me. Every year we step out of the busy schedules of our lives and take a weekend "girls trip" together, usually to a bed-and-breakfast somewhere in Texas. We spend hours laughing, sharing, and counseling. Typically one of us will lay out a problem, and the other two will offer wisdom, advice, and a few new ideas. We love it. We all agree that we come back from our little trips as better women, better mothers, and better wives.

Many times God uses the people in our lives—whether they are friends, mentors, coworkers, or family members—to give us wisdom and guidance. For women, the friendship of other women is a particularly powerful force in life, so much so that I have devoted an entire chapter later in this book (chapter 11) to the topic of friendships. I would be remiss, however, to neglect the importance of friendships in this chapter on wisdom.

Proverbs 13:20 says, "He who walks with the wise grows wise, but a companion of fools suffers harm." The truth is, friends rub off on each other, as another verse in Proverbs illustrates: "As iron sharpens iron, so one man sharpens another" (Proverbs 27:17). If we want to be wise, then it's important for us to walk through life with wise friends. If we choose to walk with foolish friends instead, we're sure to get hurt. How can we know if our friends are wise or foolish? Do a foundation check! Consider: Do they fear God and base their wisdom on a reverence for him?

Sometimes we get counsel from people who are neither friends nor family members but acquaintances or professionals. Whenever we get advice from anyone, we need to consider the source and confirm that the person giving the advice is coming from a foundation of fear and reverence of the Lord and then building on God's truth. The Bible actually gives us a checklist to help us discern whether or not we are receiving wise counsel: "But the wisdom that comes from heaven is first of all pure; then peace-loving, considerate, submissive, full of mercy and good fruit, impartial and sincere" (James 3:17). Wisdom that is none of these things is not wisdom at all.

God's Wisdom versus Man's Wisdom

There is a vast difference between God's wisdom and man's. In fact, the apostle Paul contrasts them sharply in 1 Corinthians 3:18–19 when he writes, "Do not deceive yourselves. If any one of you thinks he is wise by the standards of this age, he should become a 'fool' so that he may become wise. For the wisdom of this world is foolishness in God's sight. As it is written: 'He catches the wise in their craftiness.'" For example, the world says it's wise to watch out for Number One; God says we must think more highly of others than we do ourselves. The world says it's okay to hold a grudge and make people pay for hurting us; God says we must forgive others and leave any vengeance to him. We need to be sure we're looking for God's wisdom and not simply accepting what the world tells us is wise.

Many people confuse wisdom with knowledge. Earlier in this chapter we said that wisdom includes knowledge, but it is also much more than knowledge. In itself, knowledge is not a bad thing. H. A. Ironside said, "Scripture nowhere condemns the acquisition of knowledge. It is the wisdom of this world, not its knowledge, that is foolishness with God."[8] Wisdom tells us how to apply the knowledge we gain. Knowledge may be taught in the halls of higher learning; wisdom is *caught* as we seek it and abide in the words of our eternal God.

A story is told of a student at Columbia University who was under the impression that the institution assured he would be taught wisdom. He filed a lawsuit for eight thousand dollars based on his claim that the university had failed him in the matter. It is no surprise that the Superior Court dismissed the case, nor that the Appellate Division of the Superior Court ruled the suit had been properly dismissed. Sidney Goldmann, the presiding judge of the three-man appellate court, declared, "These charges were set in a frame of intemperate, if not scurrilous, accusations. We agree with the trial judge that wisdom is not a subject that can be taught, and that no rational person would accept such a claim made by any man or institution."[9]

Walt Whitman spoke well of the contrast between knowledge and wisdom in his *Song of the Open Road:*

Wisdom is not finally tested by the schools,

Wisdom cannot be pass'd from one having it to another not having it,

Wisdom is of the soul, is not susceptible of proof, is its own proof.[10]

There are many benefits to the pursuit of knowledge. The world rewards knowledgeable people with positions of prestige, importance, and many times affluence. But just as there are many rewards for knowledge here on this earth, there are different, more eternal rewards for wisdom. Wisdom produces a blessing that a doctorate degree cannot. Wise Solomon says,

> Blessed is the man who finds wisdom, the man who gains understanding, for she [wisdom] is more profitable than silver and yields better returns than gold. She is more precious than rubies; nothing you desire can compare with her. Long life is in her right hand; in her left hand are riches and honor. Her ways are pleasant ways, and all her paths are peace. She is a tree of life to those who embrace her; those who lay hold of her will be blessed. (Proverbs 3:13–18)

We all have heard the oft-quoted phrase, "Diamonds are a girl's best friend." But for positive women, wisdom is even more valuable. Do you love wisdom? Embrace it. Passionately pursue it from the God of wisdom himself. You will obtain blessings that are lasting and eternal in value. A woman of wisdom is truly adorned with life's greatest jewels.

POWER POINT

🌼 **Read:** The entire chapters of Proverbs 1 and 2. Make a list of the results of rejecting wisdom mentioned in this passage. What are some of the reasons people may choose to reject wisdom? Now make a second list of the benefits of pursuing wisdom. Compare the two lists.

🖤 **Pray:** God of all wisdom, how wonderful it is to go to you for wisdom, direction, and comfort! Thank you for hearing my prayers. As I pursue wisdom, help me to begin at your feet, in fear and awe of you as my wonderful Creator. Help me to grow in wisdom so that I may be a woman of wisdom and a woman of your Word. In the matchless name of Jesus I pray, amen.

Remember: "For the LORD gives wisdom, and from his mouth come knowledge and understanding" (Proverbs 2:6).

Do: Determine to pursue wisdom starting today, and begin by sitting at the feet of the Giver of wisdom, God himself. Decide on a time each day when you will read and meditate on his Word. You may choose a short Bible passage, a few verses, or a longer reading. Whatever you do, commit yourself to pulling up a chair at the banquet table of wisdom and tasting its delicious morsels daily.

Winning Wisdom
Becoming a Woman of Direction and Discretion

*Before you begin a thing, remind yourself that difficulties and
delays quite impossible to foresee are ahead....
You can only see one thing clearly, and that is your goal.*

—Kathleen Norris

Most likely you've been there: sitting in the passenger seat of the car while the driver, a male, searches for your destination for what seems like hours. Whether the guy at the wheel is your dad, your brother, your boyfriend, or your husband, the scenario is still the same. He will never admit that he is lost. Pulling over for directions is totally out of the question, and don't even try to suggest a map! "I know it's around here somewhere. I'm sure we're going in the right direction," he says. I guess it's a male ego thing, but what is so difficult about asking for help after you have been driving aimlessly for forty minutes? Let's face it, we all could use a little help with direction sometimes!

As positive women we want to be purposeful about the direction we are going and the means we use to get there. Aimlessly wandering through life will get us nowhere quickly. But how do we find our direction, our purpose, and our goals in life?

A story is told of Justice Oliver Wendell Holmes who, while traveling on a train, misplaced his ticket. Seeing that Holmes was fumbling through his pockets and belongings with mounting frustration, the conductor tried to put his mind at ease.

"Don't worry about it, Mr. Holmes," he said. "I'm sure you have your ticket somewhere. If you don't find it during the trip, just mail it in to the railroad when you reach your destination."

Holmes appreciated the kind words but was still dismayed about his predicament. He looked the conductor in the eyes and said, "Young man, my problem is not finding my ticket. It's to find out where in the world I'm going."[1]

Certainly we, too, need to have an idea of where we are going in life. Let's consider how we can find direction as we journey down life's pathways.

The Power of a Strategic Plan

Setting goals was part of my life growing up. Every New Year's Day, my dad would encourage my sister and me to take time to consider and prepare a list of our annual goals. Yearly planning was a healthy exercise for me, especially in my high school and college years. I set goals in every area of my life, from grades to body weight to spiritual growth.

My Sunday school teacher Jim Kennedy used to say, "If your target is nothing, you'll end up hitting it every time." The truth is, we need goals—and a plan of action for reaching them. They give us a vision for moving forward in our lives. Paul had this type of focus, as evidenced by what he wrote to the Philippians: "Forgetting what is behind and straining toward what is ahead, I press on toward the goal to win the prize for which God has called me heavenward in Christ Jesus" (Philippians 3:13–14).

Ultimately our goal, like Paul's, is to fulfill God's calling in our lives. As you press toward that goal, consider taking time every January 1 to write out a personal strategic plan for the next year. Your plan should be balanced in four areas: mental, physical, spiritual, and social. Be prayerful as you prepare your plan and listen for God's leading. In each area, set a specific and realistic goal that will move you toward your ultimate goal. Make each goal believable and achievable so you can really commit to it. Make it measurable, too, so you can be sure you're staying on target. Along with each goal, write specific resolutions or steps you will take to meet it.

Let's take a brief look at these four strategic areas.

Mental. Mental goals involve ways to stimulate your brain and stretch your thinking—for example, reading more books or learning a new language or working toward a degree. Whatever goal you choose, it should be measurable. If you decide to read more books, determine how many. Will you commit to reading three books a year, one book a month, a book every two weeks? Write down what is feasible for you and your current lifestyle. Push yourself, but don't discourage yourself by setting an impossible goal.

Physical. In the physical arena, you may want to consider reaching a particular weight range or dress size or cholesterol level. Write down the strategy you intend to use to achieve that goal—say, working out every other day or walking six miles per week. Other physical goals might address sleeping or eating habits. This is a good time to decide when you will make your annual doctor and dentist visits.

Spiritual. When you decide on spiritual goals, you may want to start off broad, then write down specific strategies. Let's say you want to draw closer to God and deepen your prayer life. Your strategy may be to decide on a time you will set aside to pray and meditate on God's Word each day. You may want to add other details, like where you will do this and how long each session will be. How much Scripture will you read each day? Other spiritual strategies could include joining a Bible study, volunteering at church, or meeting with a friend so you can pray together.

Social. In our fast-paced world, if we are not deliberate about getting together with friends, it may never happen. Social goals give us a plan for building relationships. Your goal may be something like "to deepen relationships with the people in my life" or "to develop more good friendships from the acquaintances I know." A specific strategy may be to invite another couple over for dinner or dessert once a month. It may be to meet a friend once a week or go away on a girls' weekend once a year. Other strategies may include hosting two parties a year or writing one note a week to a friend. Personally, I like to identify the relationships that are important to me and set a goal of seeing that person at least once a month for lunch.

Career. If you work outside the home, this additional area is for you. Perhaps you already set annual career goals at work with your staff or management; if not, spend some time praying and thinking through what you want to accomplish in the coming year. It's important that you make the goals dependent on you and not on other people. For instance, you don't want your goal to be "to get a promotion" if that's another person's decision to make. However, you can make it your goal to do everything your job requires plus more in order to put yourself in line for a promotion. Set measurable, short-term goals that will stretch you and encourage you to meet your long-term goals. Beside each goal write down three or four specific strategies you will use to help you obtain it.

As you set goals in these four or five areas, keep in mind that you can't predict the future. Some elements of the coming year are out of your immediate control. Many times, because of people or circumstances, goals have to be rearranged. Stay flexible! I think of a woman I know who had her life in order and her goals set. With both kids in school, she was ready to finish her college degree and begin a career in teaching. Until...unexpected baby number three came along and postponed her perfect plan. Of course, she was thrilled and thankful for her

He holds victory in store for the upright, he is a shield to those whose walk is blameless, for he guards the course of the just and protects the way of his faithful ones. —Proverbs 2:7–8

precious little girl! Her story reminds us that we can go ahead and make our plans; but if God has other plans, we must be flexible enough to joyfully go with God.

Trusting Him to Lead

We may not know what the future holds, but we do know the one who holds the future. Perhaps this is why Solomon tells us that if we want to find direction in life, we must trust God and not depend solely on our own insight. He says in Proverbs 3:5–6, "Trust in the LORD with all your heart and lean not on your own understanding; in all your ways acknowledge him, and he will make your paths straight." Our natural tendency is to direct our own paths according to our own understanding. But this passage says we should defer to the guidance of our omniscient God.

How can we know what is in the road ahead? How can we know what twists and turns life will bring? We can't. But we *can* know that if we trust God wholeheartedly and acknowledge him in all our ways, he will direct our paths.

Joni Eareckson Tada's life has been a journey of trust and dependence on God. As an active teenager, Joni loved life and had great plans for the future—until a diving accident in 1967 left her as a quadriplegic. In despair, she thought that her life was over. Little did she know it was only beginning.

"One of the major turning points in my life was at this time, when I was wrestling against despair and depression at the prospects of living a life of permanent paralysis without use of my hands or legs," she says. "Several good friends helped me grasp the concept of the sovereignty of God and, for me, it was life changing. It helped so much to realize that my accident was really no accident at all. Second Corinthians 4:16–18 took a new and buoyant meaning as I realized that my light and momentary afflictions could achieve for me an eternal weight of glory. The disability became a severe mercy."[2]

God led Joni to start a ministry called Joni and Friends (JAF), which reaches out and ministers to the disabled community around the world. Over the years JAF Ministries has uncovered the hidden needs of people with disabilities and has trained churches in effective outreach and ministry to this special mission field. Joni has served on the National Council on Disability and has received numerous awards and honors over the years for her tireless work on behalf of the disabled. She has authored numerous books and writes for several publications. Her five-minute radio program, "Joni and Friends," is heard daily on more than seven hundred stations.

Certainly God had great plans for Joni's life! The path he set before her may not have been the path she expected to take, but it has been a blessed path nonetheless. "When we reach beyond our comfort zones and embrace the unlikely," Joni says, "people are blessed by the realization that we are all richer when we recognize our poverty, we are strong when we see our weaknesses, and we are recipients of God's grace when we understand our desperate need of him."[3]

In my own life, two Scripture passages have helped me to trust God and embrace his plans for me. They're worth memorizing:

Jeremiah 29:11–13: "For I know the plans I have for you," declares the LORD, "plans to prosper you and not to harm you, plans to give you hope and a future. Then you will call upon me and come and pray to me, and I will listen to you. You will seek me and find me when you seek me with all your heart."

Romans 8:28: And we know that in all things God works for the good of those who love him, who have been called according to his purpose.

The Bible makes clear that our success doesn't lie in having all of the answers about our future; it lies in following God's direction day by day. The famous abolitionist Harriet Tubman revealed the secret of her success when she told her biographer, Sarah H. Bradford, in 1868, "'Twant me, 'twas the LORD. I always told him, 'I trust you. I don't know where to go or what to do, but I expect you to lead me,' and he always did."[4]

The Road Map of Life

Marge Caldwell of Houston, Texas, is a delightful speaker and writer and a wonderful woman of faith and wisdom. During my college years I had the opportunity to hear her speak, and I will never forget one of the stories she told emphasizing the importance of reading God's Word for direction. Here's my version of the story:

Fred and Dottie were a precious newlywed couple living at a navy base in Virginia. You can imagine their dismay when Fred was called into active duty during the Gulf War. In order to console sweet Dottie, Fred promised to write to her as often as possible.

Dottie anxiously waited and was absolutely thrilled when the first letter from Fred arrived in her mailbox. She looked at the envelope, ran her hands over the seal, and pressed it against her heart, knowing that the letter inside was an expression of Fred's love for her. After soaking in the perfect bliss for a while, she placed the envelope on her coffee table so that every time she walked by, she would be reminded of Fred's love.

Soon another letter arrived, and with the same thrill she kissed the envelope, held it close, and admired the handwriting on the address. It was Fred's precious handwriting! She was so happy to have received another letter, she was almost beside herself. Again she placed the envelope on the coffee table, on top of the first. Over the next several weeks, Dottie received additional letters and tenderly placed each one at the top of the mounting stack on her coffee table.

Then the glorious day came when Fred was able to call home. It was a brief call, just long enough for him to tell Dottie that he loved her and to make sure she had been receiving his letters. Dottie was thrilled to hear Fred's voice, and she assured him that indeed she had received all of his letters.

It was then that something peculiar came to light. When Fred asked Dottie if she had taken their car into the shop for an oil change, she replied, "Why no, Fred. I didn't know I was supposed to take the car into the shop."

"But Dottie," Fred said with tinge of frustration, "I told you it needed to be done in the first letter I sent to you. Didn't you read the letter?"

"Why no, Fred, I didn't read the letter," Dottie responded. "It was just so nice that you wrote me. I placed your letter on the coffee table along with the others."

Fred's voice grew more concerned. "You did deposit the check I sent, didn't you?" he asked, to which Dottie replied, "Check?"

Uh-oh. Now Fred was pretty upset, as you can imagine. He had sent numerous detailed letters to his bride, but she hadn't taken the time to read any of them. Dottie was just happy that Fred had written to her and content to keep the envelopes on the coffee table where she could see them every day. Wasn't that enough?

By now you are probably thinking that Dottie is a little nutty. Obviously this is not a true story, but in a way it is. Think about it. We have a wonderful God who has sent us a series of love letters called the Bible. This glorious book is filled with priceless treasures of wisdom as well as vital information and helpful instructions for living an abundant life. Like Dottie, many of us simply set the letters aside on the coffee table and fail to read them. It seems absurd that Dottie didn't read her letters. But isn't it more absurd that we don't read the mail sent to us by our loving heavenly Father?

In our search for direction in life, we have the privilege to turn to the very words of the all-wise Creator of the universe. Psalm 119:105 says, "Your word is a lamp to my feet and a light for my path." The Bible is our flashlight as we journey down the path of life. It leads us and guides us in truth and steers us from false and evil ways. It provides nourishment and strength along the trail. It doesn't tell us what to do in every specific situation, but it does guide us in principle. As 2 Timothy 3:16 says, "All Scripture is God-breathed and is useful for teaching, rebuking, correcting and training in righteousness, so that the man of God may be thoroughly equipped for every good work."

Knowing God's Will

A woman I know, Emily, has become increasingly dissatisfied with her job in recent months. She isn't sure if she should start looking for a new job opportunity—maybe even a whole new line of work—or stay in her current job, even though she doesn't enjoy it anymore. Wouldn't it be nice if she could open up the Bible and find a passage that says, "Emily shall move on to a new job opportunity"? But Scripture doesn't give us exact, specific directions for every decision. Thankfully, our loving heavenly Father gives us the free will to make decisions in life without being micro-managed. What Emily *can* find in the Bible is wisdom to lead her to a wise decision. She can pray, seek wise counsel from someone she trusts, and research all of her options. Then, after weighing her options and determining if any of the choices would go against a biblical principle (for example, would a particular job require her to be dishonest?), she can make her decision confidently.

Sometimes we think that there is only one perfect choice, and we must find it. If we make the wrong decision, we're doomed for life! Granted, certain life decisions do have major consequences and ramifications— like who we will marry and what career path we will take—but most decisions offer several good options. My dad used to say a simple phrase that has always stuck with me: "Make a decision, then make it a right decision." In other words, if you come to a fork in the road, after wise consideration and prayer, start walking down the path that seems the wisest; then make the best of it and leave the results to God. Once you have made a decision, work in a positive way to make it the best decision—without looking back.

People often ask the question, "How do I know if I'm in God's will?" The answer may be simpler than we think. We know we are in God's will if we are living in obedience to his Word. That's it! As we abide in him and he abides in us, our lives will be fruitful, whatever path we choose.

Often the question people are really asking is, "Which road should I take?" If we have a choice between two roads and can be obedient to God's Word on both, then God's answer is this: "I'll be with you down whatever road you choose." Most roads have challenges, twists, turns, joys, and sorrows. Just because we hit a bump or meet a roadblock doesn't mean we made a "wrong" decision— otherwise every character in the Bible went down the "wrong" road! The fact is, as we walk according to God's will, we *will* face challenges. We will have new decisions to make along the way. But as Mary Kay Ash said, "For every failure, there's an alternative course of action. You just have to find it. When you come to a roadblock, take a detour."[5]

Are you seeking direction and don't know which way to turn? Start with the road map of life, the Bible! As you pursue wisdom from above and wise counsel from people you trust, you will find that the steps in front of you become clearer. Take one step at a time. Listen to God's voice as he speaks through his Word, his people, and that still, small voice inside of you that is the Holy Spirit. You may not get the kind of exact answer that would make your decision-making process easy; but you can rest in the assurance that God is with you whatever path you take as you walk in obedience to him.

A Woman of Direction and Discretion

One of my favorite modern American heroines is Elizabeth Dole. A graduate of Duke University and Harvard Law School, Mrs. Dole served five United States presidents in an amazing career dedicated to public service. She became the first female secretary of transportation during the Reagan Administration and was appointed secretary of labor in the first Bush Administration. After completing her cabinet assignments, she became president of the Red Cross, accepting no salary during her first year in order to demonstrate the importance of volunteerism. She left the Red Cross in order to pursue the Republican nomination for president of the United States in 2000. At the time of this writing, she is running for the United States Senate, representing her home state of North Carolina.

Recently I had the opportunity to hear Mrs. Dole speak at a lecture series in Dallas. It was obvious from her speech that she is a woman of vision and direction. She moves forward, taking steps toward new opportunities that allow her to serve the country she so dearly loves. Has she faced discouragement? Yes, but she has experienced many victories as well. She doesn't look back, worrying about whether or not she made the "right" decision; she moves forward, looking toward the goal that lies ahead. She is a wonderful example of a woman of faith, wisdom, and direction.

I'm sure that Elizabeth Dole is also a woman of discretion. I can say that with confidence because discretion and wisdom go hand in hand,

Dost thou love life? Then do not squander time, for that is the stuff life is made of. —Benjamin Franklin as we see in Proverbs 8:12: "I, wisdom, dwell together with prudence; I possess knowledge and discretion." Proverbs 2:11–12 says, "Discretion will protect you, and understanding will guard you. Wisdom will save you from the ways of wicked men." Discretion can be defined as prudence, or the quality of being careful about what we say or do. It also means the freedom, power, or authority to make decisions and choices using discernment and judgment. A wise woman is always a woman of discretion!

Proverbs paints a not-so-pretty picture of a woman who lacks discretion: "Like a gold ring in a pig's snout is a beautiful woman who shows no discretion" (Proverbs 11:22). What behaviors can we expect from such a woman? The Gold Ring in the Pig's Snout award could be granted for any of the following behaviors:

- gossip
- tearing down others with words
- needless chatter (sharing too much information)
- unkind words
- corrupt communication or foul language
- temper tantrums
- angry outbursts
- adulterous flirting
- overindulgence
- wearing obviously revealing clothing

You can probably think of many more qualifications for this award, but you get the idea. Notice that most of these qualifications tend to deal with words. Unfortunately this can be a dangerous area for women, since we do enjoy talking! As one husband said, "Generally speaking, women are generally speaking." We do tend to use our mouths quite a bit, and with that comes great opportunity for error. James spoke of the power and destructive capability of the tongue in his epistle:

> The tongue is a small part of the body, but it makes great boasts. Consider what a great forest is set on fire by a small spark. The tongue also is a fire, a world of evil among the parts of the body. It corrupts the whole person, sets the whole course of his life on fire, and is itself set on fire by hell....
>
> With the tongue we praise our Lord and Father, and with it we curse men, who have been made in God's likeness. Out of the same mouth come praise and cursing. My brothers, this should not be....
>
> Who is wise and understanding among you? Let him show it by his good life, by deeds done in the humility that comes from wisdom. (James 3:5–6, 9–10, 13)

As women of wisdom, we need to live up to a higher standard, showing our wisdom through our discreet behavior and conversation. Let's determine to use our words for good. Let us not waste them putting people down, when there are so many people we can lift up! Instead, let's be positive women who have a positive influence on the people around us, choosing words and deeds that demonstrate direction, discretion, and the wisdom that comes from God.

POWER POINT

🌣 **Read:** Proverbs 31:10–31. Would you consider the woman in this passage wise? What clue is found in verse 30? List some of the activities and behaviors that indicate she is a woman of wisdom, direction, and discretion.

Pray: I praise you, Father, for your plans are perfect! You know the way that I should go. Help me to trust you and not simply lean on my own understanding. Help me to acknowledge you in all my ways as you direct my paths. I want to be a woman of wisdom, direction, and discretion, living a life that honors you in both word and deed. In Jesus' name I pray, amen.

Remember: "Charm is deceptive, and beauty is fleeting; but a woman who fears the LORD is to be praised" (Proverbs 31:30).

Do: Set aside a time to write out a strategic plan for the rest of the year. Remember to seek God's direction. As you set your goals, take some time to reflect on those areas of your life that may need a discretion tune-up. Ask God to help you have victory in these areas.

Power Principle #3

Becoming A Woman of Prayer

Devote yourselves to prayer, being watchful and thankful.

—Colossians 4:2

I know not by what methods rare,
But this I know: God answers prayer.
I know not if the blessing sought
Will come in just the guise I thought.
I leave my prayer to Him alone
Whose will is wiser than my own.

—Eliza M. Hickok

Extra Baggage
Giving Up a Load We Were Never Meant to Carry

Oh, what peace we often forfeit,
Oh what needless pain we bear,
All because we do not carry,
Everything to God in prayer.

—Joseph Scriven

Recently my sister, Karen, my stepmother, Janet, and I were on our way to Panama City, Florida, to attend the marriage of my cousin David. As we tracked from the airport terminal to our rental car, Janet and I walked briskly with our suitcases rolling along easily behind us. Karen lagged behind carrying her heavy bag. Finally in exhaustion she exclaimed, "I wish I'd brought my bag with rollers!"

Oh, the difference wheels make! Karen was carrying a load that a set of wheels could have borne. What about you and me? Are we struggling to carry our own baggage through life? By baggage I mean the troubles, problems, and challenges that are an inevitable part of human existence. The good news is, we have a God who loves us and wants to help us with our burdens. The same God who parted the Red Sea, who walked on water, and who changed water into wine is ready and willing to be our "wheels." That doesn't mean we can expect a perfect life void of pain; rather, we can rest in the assurance that we have a perfect God who loves us and is with us, whatever challenges life brings.

Don't Give Up

One of my favorite Bible verses is 1 Thessalonians 5:17: "Pray without ceasing" (NKJV). It's a short, sweet reminder that we need to give our cares and burdens to God daily. We need to continually praise him and thank him. We need to be in constant communication with him!

Theologians say this verse can be understood in two ways. I believe that both are correct. One way to "pray without ceasing" is to keep our prayer lives strong and growing. We can do this in part by designating a specific time each day to go to God in prayer with our praises and our cares. (Chapter 8 provides specific and creative ideas for having a daily prayer time.) We need to be diligent to maintain a regular, vibrant prayer life with our glorious Creator.

A second way to understand unceasing prayer is to recognize it as a constant state—a moment-by-moment, living communication with God. Brother Lawrence, who served in the kitchen of a monastery in Paris in the seventeenth century, wrote of the blessings of living in a constant state of devotion and prayer. A simple man with a humble background, his profound writings were compiled in a book called *Practicing the Presence of God,* which is still in print today. Although his job as a kitchen worker was mundane, he determined to live every moment in "the presence of God," transforming his kitchen duties into glorious experiences of heaven. Our lives can be transformed, too, when we know and experience this type of prayer-filled joy in daily living.

Jesus told his disciples a parable to illustrate to them (and to us) that they should always pray and not give up. It is found in Luke 18:2–8:

> "In a certain town there was a judge who neither feared God nor cared about men. And there was a widow in that town who kept coming to him with the plea, 'Grant me justice against my adversary.'

"For some time he refused. But finally he said to himself, 'Even though I don't fear God or care about men, yet because this widow keeps bothering me, I will see that she gets justice, so that she won't eventually wear me out with her coming!'"

And the Lord said, "Listen to what the unjust judge says. And will not God bring about justice for his chosen ones, who cry out to him day and night? Will he keep putting them off? I tell you, he will see that they get justice, and quickly."

Jesus wants us to pray. He wants us to come to him continually. Through this parable he compels us to bring our cares, concerns, burdens, and injustices to him. Unlike the judge in the story, God is just and loving, and he is waiting for us with open arms and a listening ear. He stands before us saying, "Come to me, give me your burdens, and find rest for your souls."

Is It Too Much to ASK?

I'm the type that hates to ask anyone for anything. My daughter Joy is the same way. She doesn't even like me to ask someone to give her a ride to a meeting, even when we live on the way to the meeting's location. She just hates to impose. My daughter Grace seems to have the opposite viewpoint. She assumes everyone is willing to help and doesn't mind asking for a favor at all. Her philosophy is, "They can always say no. It never hurts to ask." I suspect the healthiest approach is a balance between the two extremes.

How willing we are to ask for something is often dependent upon the person of whom we're making the request. My street is filled with wonderful, friendly neighbors. The Page family lives just across from us, and they have a daughter, Ashlee, who is in the same grade as Grace. One Friday the girls came home from school with directions for a major science project due the next Wednesday for their freshman biology class. The assignment was to make a detailed model of a living cell with all its basic parts, from mitochondrion to golgi. The only way for the girls to have it finished by Wednesday was to do the bulk of it on Saturday and Sunday.

But that happened to be the weekend I was away on my once-a-year ladies' retreat. I didn't know about the project and couldn't offer any help. Fortunately Ashlee Page invited Grace to come over so they could work on the project together. The Pages have a plentiful amount of craft supplies, and they didn't mind sharing them with Grace when she asked. By the time I arrived home on Sunday afternoon, Grace had spent a good portion of the weekend at the Pages' house, and her project was complete.

On Tuesday night, just before the project was due, Grace went over and asked the Pages if she could use their glue gun one more time. I cringed at the thought of asking one more favor from the Pages, but they were continually gracious. Believe me, I have expressed my gratitude to them many times over!

Grace's experience with the Pages is a good example of a principle that Jesus taught in the Sermon on the Mount. I call it the ASK principle, and it's found in Matthew 7:7–11:

"Ask and it will be given to you; seek and you will find; knock and the door will be opened to you. For everyone who asks receives; he who seeks finds; and to him who knocks, the door will be opened.

"Which of you, if his son asks for bread, will give him a stone? Or if he asks for a fish, will give him a snake? If you then, though you are evil, know how to give good gifts to your children, how much more will your Father in heaven give good gifts to those who ask him!"

There is a limit to human generosity. You and I don't have unlimited resources or the ability to grant every request asked of us. But God's resources and power know no limits. He is able to give abundantly more than we ask or think. What would happen in our lives if we truly applied the ASK principle—if we always remembered to ask, seek, and knock? The Greek present imperative form of the three verbs in this passage indicates that the asking, seeking, and knocking are *continuous* actions. Once again Jesus is talking about persistent prayer. What great things would take place if we prayed persistently and unceasingly to our totally unlimited, loving God?

The point of constant prayer is not so much to see what we can get from God but to build a relationship with him. Ultimately, ASKing is a continuous action of growing closer to God, seeking his ways, and increasing our faith. Let's take a look at each of the three aspects of the ASK principle.

1. *"Ask and it will be given to you."*

The word *ask* used in this verse suggests a petition made from a lesser entity to a greater one. The same word is found in Ephesians 3:20: "Now to him who is able to do immeasurably more than all we ask or imagine, according to his power that is at work within us." Again we find the word ask in Colossians 1:9: "For this reason, since the day we heard about you, we have not stopped praying for you and asking God to fill you with the knowledge of his will through all spiritual wisdom and understanding."

James used the word *ask* four times in his epistle. In James 1:5–6 we are told to ask for wisdom (as we discussed in the last chapter) and to ask for it without doubting. In James 4:2–3 we find some more instructions: "You do not have, because you do not ask God. When you ask, you do not receive, because you ask with wrong motives, that you may

Cast all your anxiety on him because he cares for you. —1 Peter 5:7 ☺

spend what you get on your pleasures." We always need to check our motives when we ask something of God. Is our request being made for selfish gain? This may be one of the reasons we don't receive it.

If our motives are right and we have a living, growing relationship with God, however, we can have confidence whenever we go to him with a request. First John 3:21–22 says, "Dear friends, if our hearts do not condemn us, we have confidence before God and receive from him anything we ask, because we obey his commands and do what pleases him." Later in John's letter we find a passage that uses the word *ask* three more times and reiterates the point: "I write these things to you who believe in the name of the Son of God so that you may know that you have eternal life. This is the confidence we have in approaching God: that if we ask anything according to his will, he hears us. And if we know that he hears us—whatever we ask—we know that we have what we asked of him" (1 John 5:13–15).

Asking of the Lord is an act of faith—one that he encourages us to do. So why are we sometimes hesitant to bring our petitions to him? Is it because we relate asking of God to the awkwardness of imposing on our fellow man? Jesus implores us to ask. Could it be we don't take the time to ask because we live too much in the here and now, always caught up in trying to solve our own problems? Jesus reminds us to ask. Do we feel unworthy, as if we do not deserve to make requests of God? Jesus lovingly tells us to ask.

Dear friend, what do you need to ask of God? Do you need wisdom? What about strength? Perhaps you need a friend. Begin asking. Start now!

2. "Seek and you will find."

The word *seek* is somewhat different than *ask*. It has to do with desiring, endeavoring, or inquiring about something. We can get a better understanding of this word by seeing how it is used in other places in the Bible. For example, Matthew 6:33 tells us to "seek first his kingdom and his righteousness, and all these things [the things we need to live and thrive in this world] will be given to you as well." Similarly, Colossians 3:1–2 tells us to set our hearts and minds "on things above...not on earthly things." In other words, our seeking ought to be geared toward eternal things. If we spend our entire lives seeking worldly riches, beauty, or fame—and that's an easy mode to slip into, since these are things we can see and feel in the here and now—whatever we obtain will be temporal; it will soon fade away. The question we need to ask ourselves is, Are we running this race of life for a temporary reward or an eternal one?

What does it mean to seek eternal things? Actually, there are only a few things that are truly eternal: God, his Word, and the souls of men. Yes, we must earn a living, live in this world, and take care of ourselves; but our real reward comes in investing in the things that won't fade away. Investing in people, drawing near to God, living according to his Word, and sharing it with others: These are activities worth seeking. In 1 Corinthians 3:1–15 Paul tells us that we are building our lives on the foundation of Christ with materials of gold, silver, and costly stones, or with wood, hay, and straw—that is, with things in life that are strong and true and have eternal value, or things that are common and temporal and ultimately flimsy. One day, he says, our works will be tested by fire. If what we have built survives, we will receive our reward.

My friend Carol is a very busy person. Besides working part-time, she volunteers at her kids' school (and with several other organizations) and leads a small-group Bible study. Carol seems to have her priorities straight when it comes to what is worth seeking and what is not. She frequently uses the phrase "hay and stubble" to refer to everything people tend to busy themselves with that is not eternal. Carol lives in a beautifully decorated house, yet she doesn't get frazzled about the details of decorating. Those are hay and stubble issues. Talk to her about the character of her kids, however, and you've got her undivided attention. She is always seeking the best for them and constantly working to enrich them. Why? Because they represent eternal souls. They are more precious than gold in her eyes.

What are you seeking? To what do you devote your heart, mind, soul, and strength? Take a moment to reflect on what you earnestly seek or strive for in life. You may find that you need to readjust your direction. Seek wisely, because you most likely will find what you are seeking!

3. "Knock and the door will be opened to you."

The Gospel of Luke presents another version of Jesus introducing the ASK principle. It is preceded by a parable about a neighbor knocking at a friend's door:

> "Suppose one of you has a friend, and he goes to him at midnight and says, 'Friend, lend me three loaves of bread, because a friend of mine on a journey has come to me, and I have nothing to set before him.'
>
> "Then the one inside answers, 'Don't bother me. The door is already locked, and my children are with me in bed. I can't get up and give you anything.' I tell you, though he will not get up and give him the bread because he is his friend, yet because of the man's boldness he will get up and give him as much as he needs.
>
> "So I say to you: Ask and it will be given to you; seek and you will find; knock and the door will be opened to you." (Luke 11:5–9)

This story is really about you and me knocking on heaven's door. The word *knock* is used figuratively to represent a persistent entreating of God for our needs. If a sinful man is willing to help a friend because

Never, never may we forget that if we would do good to the world, our first duty is to pray! —J. C. Ryle

of the friend's persistence, how much more will a loving God hear and reply? The Lord hears our pleas, he knows our needs, and he graciously receives our requests. Isn't it wonderful to know we have a Friend who is always there, ready and anxious to open the door to us?

Of course, *knocking* implies an action on our part—an action that is based on our faith in the One we are petitioning. If we are praying for a job opportunity but take no steps of action to find a job, we are not knocking. If we are praying for a better relationship with our spouse but take no positive steps to build the relationship, we are not knocking. Prayer and action go hand in hand. William Booth, the founder of the Salvation Army, said, "Work as if everything depended upon work, and pray as if everything depended upon prayer."[1] Another man put it this way: "If you want to get to the other side of the lake, you need to get in the boat and start paddling." We can be confident in taking action if we know we are praying according to God's will. The key is to be both diligent in our heartfelt prayers and faithful in our required actions.

Sometimes Wait, Sometimes No

About mid-November every year, I begin pumping my daughters for Christmas present requests. "What do you want? Make a list for me," I tell them. Now that they're teenagers, I can't assume anything; they must tell me exactly what they want. Sometimes we even go shopping together, and they pick out what they want; then I put it away until Christmas. Do they get everything they want? No!

Don't get me wrong; I don't mind their asking. In fact, I want them to put in their requests. So why don't I give them everything they ask for? Two reasons. First, overindulgence is not healthy for a child of any age. Kids must learn to wait for some things; they don't need to have everything they want right *now*. Overindulgence breeds greediness, ingratitude, impatience, and selfishness—traits I don't want to encourage in my kids. After all, the best things in life really do come to those who wait. My girls won't learn this important life lesson if I give them everything they want when they want it.

The second reason I don't grant their every request is because some things are not best for them. I love my kids and want to encourage them to grow into healthy, well-adjusted adults. There have been a few requests they have made over the years that Curt and I knew were not in their best interest, so we simply said "no."

Thankfully our loving heavenly Father doesn't give us everything we ask for either. As one of my favorite authors, C. S. Lewis, said, "If God had granted all the silly prayers I've made in my life, where should I be now?"[2] Imagine for a moment that God did give us everything we requested. Instead of a loving father, he would be a sugar daddy, meeting our every whim or desire. We would become selfish and overindulged. The course of history would be in our hands, because we could change everything with a simple request. People would come to God with only one motive: "I pray, and I get exactly what I want. What a deal!"

Isn't it good that our heavenly Father sometimes says "wait" and sometimes says "no"? Lewis also said, "Prayer is request. The essence of request, as distinct from compulsion, is that it may or may not be granted. And if an infinitely wise Being listens to the requests of finite and foolish creatures, of course He will sometimes grant and sometimes refuse them."[3]

Thankfully, answered prayer doesn't depend on our holiness or goodness. If it did, we might become prideful when God answers us or judgmental of others when their petitions aren't granted. Remember, even Christ in the Garden of Gethsemane got a "no" to his request to "let this cup pass from Me" (Matthew 26:39 NKJV). We must trust

God; he sees the eternal picture while we only see the immediate. Why does God allow a believer to suffer and die, not answering the prayers of numerous petitioners? We can't fully answer questions such as these until we get to the other side. I'm sure those people who have gone on to heaven before us are saying, "Don't worry about me. Don't weep for me. I am in a better place. My suffering was for a greater good, and now I suffer no more."

You Are Coming to a King

The story is told of Alexander the Great, who on one occasion was asked by a courtier for some financial aid. The powerful leader told the courtier to go to the treasurer and ask for whatever amount he wanted. After a little while, the treasurer appeared before Alexander. "The courtier has asked for an enormous amount of money," he reported, "and I'm hesitant to give out such an amount."

"Give him what he asks for," Alexander replied. "He has treated me like a king in his asking, and I shall be like a king in my giving!"

When I first read this story, it was accompanied by the following poem by Walter B. Knight. As positive women, we need to remember these words:

> Thou art coming to a King,
> Large petitions with thee bring;
> For His grace and power are such,
> None can ever ask too much! [4]

Many years ago there was a card on the wall of a cotton factory that read, "If your threads get tangled, send for the foreman." One day a new worker discovered that her threads had become tangled. She tried to disentangle them herself but succeeded only in making the tangle worse. Finally she sent for the foreman. When he came and looked over the situation, he asked her, "You have been doing this yourself?"

"Yes," she replied.

"But why didn't you send for me, as the instructions said?"

"I did my best," she meagerly replied.

"No, you did not," the foreman firmly stated. "Remember that doing your best is sending for me."[5]

When our lives get tangled, we are doing *our* best when we take our needs before our great Creator. Our first step is never to try to fix things ourselves; it's to go to God in prayer and seek his guidance, direction, and help. We may never know the full impact of our prayers this side of heaven. But we do know this: God wants us to ASK—and then trust him for the answer.

We can be confident that prayer changes things, because God changes things. Never underestimate the power and lasting influence of a positive woman's prayers!

POWER POINT

Read: 2 Chronicles 7:14 and Mark 1:35. As we come humbly before God, seeking his face, what does the passage in 2 Chronicles say he will do? What does the passage in Mark tell you about Jesus? If the Son of God made it a priority to pray, what should we do?

Pray: I praise you, loving and kind heavenly Father, for hearing my prayers. Thank you for encouraging me to ask of you. It is overwhelming to think that you invite simple little me to come to you, the high King of heaven. I humbly draw before your throne of grace. In faith I reach out to you, offering my love, my obedience, and my requests. Thank you for answering my prayers in the way you know is best for me. In Christ's holy name I pray, amen.

💡 **Remember:** "Ask and it will be given to you; seek and you will find; knock and the door will be opened to you. For everyone who asks receives; he who seeks finds; and to him who knocks, the door will be opened" (Matthew 7:7–8).

☺ **Do:** Apply the ASK principle in your life starting today. Put small, motivating signs around your home that say, "Remember to ASK." Begin each day with prayer; then in every situation that day, before fretting or becoming discouraged, pray and ask for God's help and direction. Make this a moment-by-moment practice, walking hand in hand with God throughout the day.

A Simple Guide to Effective Prayer
Praying for Family, Friends, and the World

The prayer of a righteous man is powerful and effective.

—James 5:16

Sir Isaac Newton, famous discoverer of the law of universal gravitation, was gifted as a mathematician, scientist, and philosopher. He formulated the three laws of motion, advanced the discipline of dynamics, and helped develop the study of calculus. He laid the foundation for the law of energy conservation and constructed the first reflecting telescope. His profound intellect never diminished his deep faith, however. In fact, using the telescope as an illustration, he gave us a beautiful picture of prayer: "I can take my telescope and look millions and millions of miles into space; but I can lay my telescope aside, go into my room and shut the door, get down on my knees in earnest prayer, and I see more of heaven and get closer to God than I can when assisted by all the telescopes and material agencies on earth."[1]

Isn't it wonderful to realize that the God of the universe is close at hand? We don't have to travel to distant lands or the deepest regions of space to find our great and mighty Creator. As Newton said, it's in earnest prayer that we see heaven and get close to God.

There is no secret scientific formula for prayer. Prayer is simple. It is a humble coming to God with a heart of praise, thankfulness, and need. In the last chapter we said that the main purpose of prayer is not to get God to give us things, but rather to grow with him in a deeper, more intimate relationship. I like how Hank Hanegraaff puts it in his book *The Prayer of Jesus:* "For Christians, prayer should be its own reward. Prayer is not a magic formula to get things from God. Communing with God in prayer is itself the prize."[2]

Prayer is not for show or for the applause of men, but for intimacy with the Father. I think of the story of the little girl who was saying her nightly prayers with her mother sitting next to her on the bed. The young girl's lips were moving, her expression was earnest, but the mother could barely make out what she was saying. When the little girl said, "Amen," her mother commented, "Honey, I didn't hear a word you said." Her daughter answered, "That's okay, I wasn't talking to you anyway."[3] Our prayers are very real, meaningful conversations between meager mankind and our glorious God. Aren't you overwhelmed at the thought of it?

In this chapter I want to deal with the nitty-gritty of prayer—the how, when, what, and where of prayer. Let's begin with the question "How do we learn to pray?"

Lord, Teach Us to Pray

The disciples asked Jesus this very question. One day, after Jesus had finished praying in a certain place, one of the disciples said to him, "Lord, teach us to pray." Matthew 6:9–13 gives us Jesus' response:

"This then, is how you should pray:
'Our Father in heaven,
hallowed be your name,
your kingdom come,
your will be done

on earth as it is in heaven.

Give us today our daily bread.

Forgive us our debts,

    as we also have forgiven our debtors.

And lead us not into temptation,

but deliver us from the evil one.' "

Jesus gave this model for prayer to his disciples and to us. How wonderful to learn the principles of prayer from Jesus himself! Just as in school we have the three R's (reading, writing, and arithmetic), so in this prayer we see three R's emerging: recognize who he is; remember what he has done; request according to his will. Let's take a brief look at each of these prayer principles in light of Jesus' example prayer.

Recognize who he is. Jesus began his prayer with the words, "Our Father in heaven, hallowed be your name." This statement makes very clear to whom we pray. We pray to God, our Father in heaven—not to angels or people who have gone before us. The phrase "in heaven" reminds us of God's glory and majesty. Psalm 103:19 says, "The LORD has established his throne in heaven, and his kingdom rules over all." For believers, this throne is a throne of grace. Because of Jesus' death on the cross, we have ready access to God's presence in heaven.

The term *hallowed* means holy, set apart, sanctified. When we come to God in prayer, we not only recognize that he is our loving Father in heaven, but also that his name is holy, pure, powerful. It is a name to be respected and revered. His name provides a place of safety for us, as we read in Proverbs 18:10: "The name of the LORD is a strong tower; the righteous run to it and are safe." Do you find safe refuge in him through prayer? Run to the strong tower of his holy name and find peace!

Remember what he has done. Once we reflect and begin to recognize the greatness of God, our hearts overflow with thankfulness for what he has done. Surely he is at work in big and small ways in our lives! One person put it this way: "God's giving deserves our thanksgiving." Vincent de Paul said, "We should spend as much time in thanking God for his benefits as we do in asking him for them."[4] I don't know about you but I'm a little convicted by that statement. If we spent more time in gratitude and less time in grumbling, I wonder how different our world would be.

Paul says we should "give thanks in all circumstances, for this is God's will for you in Christ Jesus" (1 Thessalonians 5:18). Thanking God for the good things in our lives is easy. Thanking him for the challenges—now that's a different story! But we have much to be thankful for, even when life is difficult. We can begin by thanking God that he is with us in our circumstances. We may not like the situation, but we can thank him for his strength and his help to make it through. As positive women, let's determine today to spend more time thanking God and reflecting on his work in our lives. I have a feeling we'll begin to see a difference in our attitude toward life as well.

Request according to his will. Jesus' model prayer goes on to present several petitions before the Lord. This section begins, however, by deferring to God's will. How do we know we are praying according to God's will? By praying according to his Word. George Mueller, the great prayer warrior of England, always consulted Scripture before petitioning God. At times he spent days searching the Scriptures before asking God for a request, because he wanted to be sure that his prayer request was in the will of God.

Madame Jeanne Guyon, born in France in 1648, was a humble yet positive woman of prayer. At the age of fifteen she married an invalid who was twenty-three years her senior. He was a rather difficult man; yet throughout her unhappy marriage, she found respite in her devo-

Satan trembles when he sees the weakest saint upon his knees. —William Cowper

tional life. Later Jeanne lived in a convent under royal order for a year. She was eventually imprisoned in Vincennes because her religious beliefs differed from the established church. She spent almost twenty-five years of her life in confinement, and many of her books were written during that period.

Madame Guyon's writings compel readers to experience God at a deeper level. In her book *Experiencing the Depths of Jesus Christ* (sometimes titled *A Short and Very Easy Method of Prayer*), she talks about a wonderful way to pray. She writes, "'Praying the Scripture' is a unique way of dealing with the Scripture; it involves both reading and prayer. Turn to the Scripture; choose some passage that is simple and fairly practical. Next, come to the Lord. Come quietly and humbly. There, before him, read a small portion of the passage of Scripture you have opened to. Be careful as you read. Take in fully, gently, and carefully what you are reading. Taste it and digest it as you read."[5]

I love that descriptive phrase "Taste it and digest it." It reminds me of Psalm 34:8, which says, "Taste and see that the Lord is good; blessed is the man who takes refuge in him." If we know that the LORD is good, we will be more likely to trust him and submit our will to his. Jesus said, "If you remain in me and my words remain in you, ask whatever you wish, and it will be given you" (John 15:7). As we taste and digest God's Word, we come to know God's will, and we are better able to pray according to it.

Prayer Requests

We can learn a lot from looking at the specific petitions in Jesus' model prayer. When we pray, "Give us this day our daily bread," for example, we are acknowledging that God is the supplier of our daily needs. How easy it is for us to look ahead and worry about tomorrow! But God wants us to trust him and look to him for provision day by day.

When we pray, "Forgive us our debts as we forgive our debtors," we are recognizing the significant role of forgiveness in a believer's life. Forgiveness is a very important concept to God. Certainly the Bible teaches about it often (see Matthew 18:21–35; 2 Corinthians 2:10; Ephesians 4:32; Colossians 3:13). We ought to value forgiveness highly as well. Why should we forgive? Because we have no right to hold something over another person when God has forgiven us our entire debt of sin. We must not let unforgiveness ruin our lives! (We will talk more about forgiving others in chapter 11.)

When we pray, "Do not lead us into temptation, but deliver us from the evil one," we are asking God not only to steer us away from temptations but also to give us the strength to stand against them. The Old Testament character Jabez prayed a similar prayer when he asked "that Your hand would be with me, and that You would keep me from evil, that I may not cause pain!" (1 Chronicles 4:10 NKJV). Do we sincerely pray that God will lead us away from temptation, or do we dabble near temptation, forgetting to ask for God's help? May our daily cry be for God's leading and deliverance!

Jesus closes his sample prayer with another acknowledgment of who God is and how great he is: "For yours is the kingdom and the power and the glory forever." When we pray these or similar words, we are making a statement of faith. We are confirming that we believe God can do all things, including answering our prayers. We are making a profound statement that erupts from a heart of faith. Let's make it our daily proclamation!

For Whom Do We Pray?

Mrs. B lives next door. She is a kind, lovely lady with grown children whose life has taken several significant and difficult turns in the last few years. Her husband left her, she was diagnosed with cancer, and she requires regular chemotherapy treatments. Several gracious women in our neighborhood who also have grown children have joined together to take turns driving Mrs. B to the hospital and back. What a beautiful picture of compassion as her neighbors surround her with love!

Wondering what I could do for Mrs. B, I asked her son if I could bring meals. He told me his mother felt sick to her stomach so often that she probably wouldn't be able to eat much food. Visiting time was limited because her energy was zapped, and she spent much of the day resting. With that option out, it occurred to me that I could be a messenger of encouragement to Mrs. B by sending her notes, books, and gifts. And I could give her an even greater gift: I could faithfully pray for her.

It is easy to think that prayer is a small thing to do for someone, when in fact it is the most powerful and positive thing we can do for another human being. We should never downplay its value. J. C. Ryle said, "Never, never may we forget that if we would do good to the world, our first duty is to pray!" Have you wondered what you could do for the families of the victims of September 11? Pray that they know God's love and strength and that they feel his arms of comfort around them. Are you concerned about the burn patient you know in the ICU? Pray for God's help and healing, both physical and emotional. Have you tried to help a friend in a troubled marriage, to no avail? Pray for God to work in ways you can't even imagine. Always do what you can to help others, but make sure your prayers are included in your help.

Remembering to pray for everyone in our lives and for everyone who is in need may seem like a monumental task. I have found it helpful to break down my prayer requests by praying for certain people or groups of people on certain days of the week. Of course there are people I pray for every single day, such as the members of my family.

I pray every day for immediate needs. But here's how I schedule prayer time for the other people I want to pray for on a regular basis:

- Sunday—Pray for preachers, missionaries, and others in ministry

- Monday—Pray for my extended family, sister, in-laws, and cousins

- Tuesday—Pray for America, the president, and other national leaders

- Wednesday—Pray for world leaders and people in different lands

- Thursday—Pray for those who are sick, hurting, and suffering, both near and abroad

- Friday—Pray for friends, their families, their marriages, and their needs

- Saturday—Pray for the surrounding community, civic leaders, and teachers

You may want to make up your own schedule, one that covers all of the prayer bases that are important to you. Many resources are available to help you pray for different groups or needs. Zondervan's *Operation World: The Day by Day Guide to Praying for the World* by Patrick Johnstone is a book that provides information about every country in the world and how you can pray specifically for the people of each nation. At www.Roaring-Lambs.org you can find a prayer guide for praying for the governors and leaders of each state in our nation week by week. In *The Power of a Positive Mom,* I included a list of specific and scriptural areas of prayer for your family. But remember, the best resource of all is God's Holy Spirit within you, as Romans 8:26 says: "In the same way, the Spirit helps us in our weakness. We do not know what we ought to pray for, but the Spirit himself intercedes for us with groans that words cannot express." God knows the names and the needs, even if you don't. Your part is to be faithful to pray.

Finding the Best Time to Pray

You may be like me. If I don't put something down on my schedule, it won't happen. That's why it's important for me to place prayer on my daily docket of activities. If I do not deliberately set aside a time for prayer, the day will fly by, and my prayer time will disappear as well.

Jesus purposefully went out early in the morning and prayed, as Mark 1:35 notes. Certainly we can pray throughout the day, here and there, and we should. But it is also important to plan a deliberate meeting with God. The great Martin Luther once said, "I am so busy now that I find if I did not spend two or three hours each day in prayer, I could not get through the day. If I should neglect prayer but a single day, I should lose a great deal of the fire of faith."[6] Okay, okay. Maybe you and I can't pray two or three hours a day. But you get Luther's point!

When is the best time to pray during the day? The psalmist said, "In the morning, O LORD, you hear my voice; in the morning I lay my requests before you and wait in expectation" (Psalm 5:3). There are a number of good reasons to meet God in the morning. Nevertheless each of us should determine what time is best for our own schedules. I personally love getting up early in the morning before anyone else in the house is awake. I grab my cup of coffee and enjoy those quiet moments with my loving heavenly Father. How wonderful it is to enjoy the sunrise with its Maker!

Morning offers me the opportunity to lay my cares before the Lord; then I don't have to worry about them during the day. I ask the Lord to order my day from the very start, so I will be able to use my time to the fullest. I also ask God to make me aware of people's needs and direct my steps so I can be a vessel of his love and care. I find that meeting God in the morning gives me an eternal perspective on the circumstances that occur throughout the day.

You are never so high as when you are on your knees. —Jean Hodges

Where's Your Secret Spot?

My giant dog, Bear, has a favorite spot in the house. The full-length windows in our living room at the front of the house offer the perfect guard post for our Great Pyrenees. This oversized white ball of fluff rests at his spot throughout the day, laying his head on the window sill and peering out at the neighborhood. All is right with the world when Bear is in his spot! Do you have a spot—a favorite place to read the paper or a beloved book? Having a spot for prayer is a good idea too. A solitary place, similar to the kind to which Jesus often withdrew. A place where you can be alone to converse with God. Keep a Bible, a blank journal, and a pen at your spot so you'll have them ready, and use the prayer journal to write your thoughts, praises, and requests to God.

Think of this spot as your special meeting place with God, just as you may have a special restaurant or coffee shop or park bench to meet your best friend. Your prayer spot may be a couch near the window, a small room away from the hustle and bustle of home life, or even a large closet. It may be helpful to inform other family members that when you are in this spot, there is an invisible "do not disturb" sign; this is your time alone with God.

In my high school years I began to recognize my need for solitude in prayer, so I used my walk-in closet as my prayer place. My parents knew if they couldn't find me anywhere else, I could possibly be in there. Using a closet for prayer may sound silly, but it is actually biblical! In the Sermon on the Mount, Jesus addresses the importance of praying in secret: "But you, when you pray, go into your inner room [*closet* in the King James Version], close your door and pray to your Father who is in secret, and your Father who sees what is done in secret will reward you" (Matthew 6:6 NASB).

My friend Carol Regehr recognized her need for a special time alone with God and wanted an "inner room" in which to pray. She finally found the perfect spot: a space between two unused clothing racks in her master bedroom closet. Understand, Carol lives in Texas, where everything is big—and that includes most closets. Carol's closet had just the perfect amount of unused space, so she hung white lace curtains on the metal rods and turned it into her sacred spot to meet with the Lord.

Wanting to put a desk and chair in her inner room, she began praying that God would lead her to the perfect little desk. Her husband assured her she'd never find a desk small enough to fit in the closet area, but Carol persisted in prayer and hunting. One day she happened to walk by an antique store, and guess what she saw in the window? The perfect desk! Her husband even came to the store with measuring tape to be quite sure of the dimensions. It truly was a perfect fit—and a gift from God. Carol says her prayer time in her special, homemade prayer closet is the secret to her peaceful and joyful life.

Of course with prayer, the place is not as important as the heart. No matter where our special place is, we must come with an open heart and a listening ear. Prayer is not just a time to read out our list of requests and be done with it, like a visit to Santa Claus at the mall. We need to listen too. Can you imagine meeting with a dear friend every day and never giving your friend a chance to say anything? A good relationship is based on communication from both parties.

How does God speak to us? Perhaps through a passage of Scripture he leads us to in the Bible. Perhaps through a still, small voice as we sit quietly before him. As we commune with God, we truly begin to abide in him. Our relationship becomes rich and full. We become less worrisome and more faithful. The time we spend with him will be evident in our peace and joy.

Hannah Whitall Smith lived a life of joy in the Lord. She is the author of *The Christian's Secret of a Happy Life*, a book that has sold more than three million copies since it was first published in 1870. It is considered one of the great classics in Christian literature. According to Hannah, the secret to a happy life is to trust completely in the promises of God's Word. She shares this story concerning prayer:

> The story was of a poor woman who had been carried triumphantly through a life of unusual sorrow. She was giving the history of her life to a kind visitor on one occasion, and at the close, the visitor said feelingly, "I do not see how you could bear so much sorrow!"
>
> "I did not bear it," was the quick reply; "the Lord bore it for me."
>
> "Yes," said the visitor, "that is the right way. We must take our troubles to the Lord."
>
> (The poor woman replied) "We must do more than that; we must leave them there. Most people take their burdens to him, but they bring them away with them again, and are just as worried and unhappy as ever, but I take mine and I leave them with him, and come away and forget them. I do this over and over, until at last I just forget I have any worries."[7]

Do you want to live a happier, more joyful Christian life? Learn to give your worries to God in prayer. To make it easier, consider trying something I first learned to do in high school. Make a small "prayer box." A simple shoebox will do, and you can decorate it if you like. Then, when you have a care or worry, write out a prayer to God about that concern on a small piece of paper. Place the paper in the prayer box and leave it there as a physical reminder that you have given the matter over to God, and you are not to worry about it yourself.

Of course, as we discussed earlier in chapter 7, it's important to be persistent in prayer. But persistence based on trust and faith in God's ability to answer us is not the same as worrying. When we offer a concern to God, it is no longer ours. The issue and its resolution are now in his hands—and we can rest in the assurance that he is big enough to handle any care that comes our way.

Oh the joy of releasing all our worries to him! A positive woman is one who knows this secret of a happy Christian life. Let's commit ourselves to becoming women of faithful, daily prayer, and watch how our lives—and the lives of those around us—fill up with the peace and joy of God.

POWER POINT

⚙ **Read:** Psalm 116. What reason does the psalmist have to be elated? Have you ever been overflowing with joy as you've seen God work in your life? Did you share your gratitude with God and with others? Will you do as David did and share the thrill of answered prayer in the future?

♡ **Pray:** Wonderful Lord, loving heavenly Father, thank you for allowing me to bring my burdens to you each day. How marvelous you are to listen to my requests! I confess that I often try to carry too many burdens and worries on my own. Help me to give these cares over to you on a daily basis. Help me to be faithful to meet with you and enjoy the sweet fellowship of your love, your Word, and your presence. In Jesus' loving name, amen.

💡 **Remember:** "Enter his gates with thanksgiving and his courts with praise; give thanks to him and praise his name. For the LORD is good and his love endures forever; his faithfulness continues through all generations" (Psalm 100:4–5).

☺ **Do:** Decide today on a time and a place where you will meet with the Lord in prayer. Begin the time by reading Scripture and praising God, thanking him for his care. Then share your needs with him. Take time to listen to him too.

Power Principle #4

Becoming A Woman of Joy

For the joy of the LORD is your strength.

—Nehemiah 8:10

Joy is not a luxury or a mere accessory in the Christian life.
It is the sign that we are really living in God's wonderful love,
and that love satisfies us.

—Andrew Murray

Experiencing Joy
Finding Bright Skies in a Dark World

Christianity is the most encouraging, the most joyous,
the least repressive of all the religions of mankind.
While it has its sorrows and stern disciplines,
the end of it is a resurrection, not a burial—a festival, not a funeral.

—L. P. Jacks

What makes you happy? Your answer to that question may fluctuate throughout life. When I was a teenager, my list of things that made me happy went something like this:

- A trip to Six Flags Amusement Park with my best friend

- An *A* in chemistry

- Giggling with friends at a slumber party

- A phone call from a certain boy

- A smile of approval from my mother and/or dad

- Going to the mall with my sister

- A fun date

- Playing with my dog Fritz

- Eating a Fletcher's Corny Dog at the Texas State Fair

- Going to the movies

- Going on a chapel choir tour

Now that I'm forty-something, my happiness list looks a little different. Here's the current list:

- A cup of hot tea and a good book on a rainy day
- Lunch with friends (and of course, still giggling)
- A smile from my husband
- Quality time with my daughters doing what they want to do
- A date with my husband at a quiet restaurant
- A Caribbean cruise with family and friends
- Prayer time with my girlfriends
- Writing for hours at a time
- Going to the movies with another couple, and dessert afterward
- Watching my kids perform in athletics or on stage
- Snuggling up with my husband
- Hugging my kids
- Long family walks

What does your happiness list look like? You may want to take a moment to write it out. It's actually fun to reflect on happy moments and think about what really makes you feel warm and fuzzy. The interesting thing about happiness is that it is a *dependent* quality. It depends on people and circumstances. If things are nice and pleasant and people are kind, then we'll be happy. If events don't run smoothly or people are rude, then happiness seems to flutter away. Happiness is nice, but it's temporary. Here today, gone tomorrow.

Joy is something different altogether. Joy is a constant. It's not dependent on circumstances or people but rather on a heart issue. Happiness is external; joy is internal. Joy can be tucked deep in the heart, even in difficult circumstances. We have a tendency to hope that joy will come to us, and we often pursue a variety of pleasures to get it—from shopping to eating to extramarital affairs. But if we are looking for pleasure and hoping to find joy, we are wasting our time. Joy dwells within and cannot be secured with outward things.

Where Is Joy?

In the Bible *joy* is used as both a noun and a verb. The noun *joy* means "delight or gladness." We see it used in Acts 2:28: "You have made known to me the paths of life; you will fill me with joy in your presence." We find *joy* in the verb form in Habakkuk 3:18: "Yet I will rejoice in the LORD, I will joy in the God of my salvation" (NKJV). I am actually overwhelmed at the number of verses that speak about joy in the Bible. In my exhaustive concordance I found more than 180 verses mentioning joy. I'm exhausted just counting them!

If God speaks so much about joy, then why don't more Christians experience it? Like a "Where's Waldo" picture, picking out a joyful Christian in certain groups of believers can be hard. It shouldn't be that way! As women of faith, our joy can and should be evident. I wonder what the effect would be on the unbelieving world if they could see the evidence of joy in our lives on a daily basis. The German philosopher Friedrich Nietzsche said scornfully about Christians of his day, "I would believe in their salvation if they looked a little more like people who have been saved."[1] Ouch, that hurts! Surely those of us who have tasted God's abundant love, his everlasting forgiveness, and his glorious mercy ought to be radiating an overwhelming joy!

What does joy look like? Is it a glowing expression and a delightful smile? It can be. But while our facial expressions are certainly one way we express the joy in our hearts, there are times in our lives when we may have joy without a smile. Then, evidence of our joy may be found in our words. Words of kindness, gratitude, and praise represent a joyful heart, while words of gossip, grumbling, and complaining reflect quite the opposite. Joy may also be evident in our actions. Joy spreads encouragement and hope; it delights in the Lord and his work; it is glad when his righteousness wins out.

The opposite of joy is not necessarily sorrow, for we can be sorrowful over a situation yet still have a deep, abiding joy. No, the opposite of joy is the state of being restless, discouraged, hopeless, and discontent. I'd rather be joyful, wouldn't you? The fact is, a positive woman is a joyful woman, and a joyful woman has a powerful effect on the people around her. Joy is a magnet that draws people to God's love, hope, and forgiveness.

Got Joy?

Don't you just love the advertisements from the dairy industry showing various distinguished celebrities with more than enough evidence on their faces to prove they have been drinking milk? The dairy farmers are hoping these ads will make us want to drink more milk from their favorite source, the cow. Hey, if Mr. Celebrity loves milk, then I want to drink it, too! The caption always reads, "Got milk?"

I have a different caption for Christians: "Got joy?" In other words, is the evidence of joy obvious in our lives? What kind of advertisements are we? Are people drawn to God because of our joy? What is the source of our joy? To answer that last question, let's take a quick "joy jog" through the Bible and see what the Scriptures reveal about the source of a believer's joy:

- Psalm 35:9: "Then my soul will rejoice in the LORD and delight in his salvation."

- Psalm 43:4: "Then will I go to the altar of God, to God, my joy and my delight."

The deepest wishes of the heart find expression in secret prayer. —George E. Rees

138

- Isaiah 61:10: "I delight greatly in the LORD; my soul rejoices in my God. For he has clothed me with garments of salvation and arrayed me in a robe of righteousness."

- Luke 1:46–47: "And Mary said: 'My soul glorifies the Lord and my spirit rejoices in God my Savior.'"

- John 15:11: "I have told you this so that my joy may be in you and that your joy may be complete.

- Romans 5:11: "Not only is this so, but we also rejoice in God through our Lord Jesus Christ, through whom we have now received reconciliation."

- Philippians 4:4: "Rejoice in the Lord always. I will say it again: Rejoice!"

Did you notice that joy is closely connected to salvation? Christians have a joy and delight that unbelievers cannot experience. It is the joy of knowing that our sins are forgiven and our lives are made new through God's gift of his Son, Jesus. We ought to sing along with the psalmist (who looked to God for his salvation), "But I trust in your unfailing love; my heart rejoices in your salvation. I will sing to the LORD, for he has been good to me" (Psalm 13:5). He has been good to us! *Rejoice!*

Even now God is at work in our lives through the Holy Spirit, producing "fruit" such as love, joy, peace, patience, kindness, goodness, faithfulness, gentleness, and self-control (Galatians 5:22–23). Do we strive and work for this fruit? No, the fruit is the work of the Holy Spirit. Jesus tells us that if we abide in him and he abides in us, then we will bear much fruit; but without him we can do nothing (see John 15:4). So the question arises: If joy is something we receive from the Lord, do we have any responsibility in obtaining it?

Yes, joy is a gift from God, but we must make the decision to experience it. Paul instructed the believers at Thessalonica, "Be joyful always" (1 Thessalonians 5:16), implying that joy is an act of will. In numerous letters Paul tells his readers to rejoice. God gives us joy, and we must act upon it.

Think of it this way. Imagine that a large, colorful package is delivered to your door. The courier tells you the box is filled with wonderful gifts that will bless you and everyone around you. You bring it inside and set it in the middle of the living room. You plan to open it, but you figure you will wait until your life is a little better, a little more settled, with fewer problems. So there the package sits, waiting to be opened. It's your gift; it belongs to you, but you're just not ready to open it. "Life's too busy," you say. Or perhaps you say, "There are people in my life right now who hurt me or make me angry. When they go away, I'll open the package." Or, "My job makes me miserable. I'll open the box when I find the perfect job." Or, "I don't feel well. When I am out of this physical pain, I'll open it." So the present sits unopened.

Many of us fail to unwrap the box, and we use a variety of excuses in our defense. "My childhood was miserable, so I can't experience joy." "My husband is awful, so I can't rejoice in the Lord." To one degree or another, we all need to go through and weed out our excuses by confessing our unforgiveness toward others. By releasing the bitterness that has crowded out any hope of joy. By recognizing that no one is perfect, including us. By relinquishing the hurt and pain we've grown strangely accustomed to. By applying God's healing salve of forgiveness.

Let's choose joy instead of bitterness. The people who anger us or the circumstances that annoy us should not darken the joy within us. Jesus prepared his disciples for his coming death by telling them, "Now is your time of grief, but I will see you again and you will rejoice [speaking of his resurrection], and no one will take away your joy" (John 16:22). Remember, no one can take away the joy we have in Christ!

That's assuming, of course, we have opened the package. What will we find inside? The promise of eternal life, for one thing. Can you imagine how joyless life would be if we didn't have the hope of spending eternity with God? Also inside are other amazing gifts such as forgiveness, freedom from guilt, salvation, and the right to become "children of God" (John 1:12). Each of these and more have been prepared for us by our loving heavenly Father. Joy is born as we accept his gift and grow in our relationship with him. Joy erupts as we enjoy his presence and follow his will. Joy overflows as we serve others and allow God's love to pour through us.

All this joy is available, just waiting to be accessed! Let's choose to open the gift of joy and watch the blessings flow out. Joy is one of those gifts that keeps on giving. When we open the gift of joy in our hearts, it will always overflow to those around us.

*Son*shine behind the Clouds

Please understand that Paul's instruction to "rejoice always" does not diminish the necessity of mourning or grieving. There are times in each of our lives when we face pain, disappointment, and loss, whether great or small. The death of a loved one, the suffering of an innocent child, the pain of divorce—these are reasons for deep sadness and sorrow, and rightly so. We must cry. Just as we should rejoice with those who rejoice, we must weep with those who weep (see Romans 12:15). Having joy doesn't negate grief. Real joy, after all, is not a surface-type happiness. Joy and sorrow *can* coexist.

You may be asking, "But where is the joy when life gets difficult? If it's there, why can't I see it?" Think about the sky on a stormy day.

Although the clouds cover up the sun, the sun is still there. It hasn't left and gone to another solar system. We can't see it, but it is there; it's just hidden. The good news is that as the clouds break up—and they always do—the sunshine returns to full view. In difficult times our joy may not be visible on the outside, but it's still there on the inside. It hasn't left.

Joy is more than a feeling; it is a deep peace, blended together with a solid hope that God has not left us. Joy is a delight in knowing there will be a better day. Can we have joy as our companion even when the road gets bumpy? Absolutely. James made a shocking contrast when he wrote, "Consider it pure joy, my brothers, whenever you face trials of many kinds, because you know that the testing of your faith develops perseverance. Perseverance must finish its work so that you may be mature and complete, not lacking anything" (James 1:2–4).

Many examples throughout history attest to the presence of joy even in the midst of sorrow. In my own life, I grieved when my mother, Barbara Kinder, was tragically killed at age fifty-five. My father, my sister, my husband, and my kids were shocked and saddened beyond belief. Yet we all experienced a peaceful joy knowing that Mom was in heaven with the Lord. I can't explain it. It wasn't a joy with a happy face; it was a peace deep within our hearts. We knew that we knew that God loves our family, and he had his loving arms wrapped around us. This kind of joy doesn't come from just knowing about God. It comes from experiencing him in our lives.

Kathleen is a woman who has experienced "*Son*shine"—the joy of the Lord—in the midst of dark circumstances. Most likely you will never see her on television or read about her in the newspaper; but like many heroes of the faith who will have great rewards in heaven, she has lived a humble life here on earth. Her granddaughter, Lisa Flagg, shares this account of her life:

In 1939, when she was twenty-eight years of age, Kathleen's husband left her and her five children who ranged in age from two to ten. Living in East Texas with no money and meager job opportunities, her future and that of her children looked very bleak. The first work she could find was in the fields at local farms. Soon she found a job cooking meals for the little community school in their area.

Rather than despair and give in to bitterness, she accepted her lot and moved forward. She never gave in to self-pity. The family endured years of true poverty, often having only a little food of the simplest kind. She kept the family together and raised all five children to responsible adulthood. A testimony to her success is the closeness of our family to this day. Growing up I never heard her complain about her circumstances in those early years or speak ill of the husband who left her to endure such hardship. That kind of life makes an impact!

Whenever we ask about that long and awful period in her life, she responds with unselfconscious frankness: "I didn't have a choice. I had five children to care for, and I was too busy doing what I could to dwell on how things could be or should be." But my grandmother did have a choice. She could have chosen despair and self-pity, which only drains initiative and will. I'm thankful she chose to face her problems and deal with them. She always reminds us that she "prayed a lot" and trusted that God was in control and could see them through.

Because of her faith, courage, and positive attitude, my grandmother has been a very strong influence in my life. If I ever find myself overwhelmed by difficult circumstances or seem to be slipping into self-pity during a hardship or unpleasant time, I think of my grandmother and say to myself, "I have it easy! Look at what Nannie endured and survived"—and I am revived![2]

If you obey my commands, you will remain in my love, just as I have obeyed my Father's commands and remain in his love. I have told you this so that my joy may be in you and that your joy may be complete. —John 15:10–11

143

Kathleen is a testimony to God's strength, peace, and joy—not a giddy schoolgirl-type of joy, but the type of joy that runs deep within the soul. The type of joy that looks beyond the problems and sees God in the solution. The type of joy that is spoken of in Hebrews 12:2: "Let us fix our eyes on Jesus, the author and perfecter of our faith, who for the joy set before him endured the cross, scorning its shame, and sat down at the right hand of the throne of God."

Greater Joy Up Yonder

As positive women and believers in Christ, we can look forward to an even greater joy: the joy of seeing Jesus face to face one day. We may find ourselves in a difficult situation or feel like we've been handed a terrible lot in life, but as Christians we can always look forward to the joy down the road. A day will come when all sorrow and pain will cease. Psalm 30:5 says, "Weeping may remain for a night, but rejoicing comes in the morning." D. L. Moody put it this way: "This is the land of sin and death and tears…but up yonder is unceasing joy!"[3] We take joy in the anticipation of that great day!

The story is told of a Christian lady who frequently visited an old, bedridden saint who always seemed to be cheerful despite her circumstances. This visitor had a wealthy friend who also professed to be a believer but was constantly looking at the dark side of things. Thinking it would do her glum friend good, she brought her on the next visit to the old woman's fifth-story apartment.

Climbing the stairs, the two friends reached the first story of the building. At that point the rich lady held her dress high off the ground and said, "How dark and filthy it is!"

"It's better higher up," said her friend.

They got to the next story, which was no better than the first. The rich lady complained again, but her friend replied, "It's better higher up."

At last they got to the fifth story. When they entered the sickroom, the rich woman saw a lovely carpet on the floor, flowering plants on the window sill, and birds singing from the roof outside. There they found the bedridden woman—one of those saints God is polishing for a greater kingdom—beaming with joy.

"It must be very hard for you to lie here," the wealthy woman said.

The sweet saint simply smiled and said, "It's better higher up."[4]

Truly one of these ladies was very rich indeed! She was rich with an eternal joy, because her mind and heart looked forward to a better day. It's so easy to sweat the small stuff and groan over our immediate cares and concerns; but as we turn our sights heavenward, we gain a whole new perspective. In this life we are going to have happy times and sad times. But at all times, we can be positive, joyful women because we have our heavenly Father's assurance: "It's better higher up."

POWER POINT

Read: Luke 10:38–42. Which of the two women in this passage seemed to experience joy? Describe Martha's main focus and then describe Mary's main focus. Which description fits you best?

Pray: Glorious heavenly Father, you are the Giver of joy. I praise you for the joy of my salvation. Oh, how wonderful to know that I am forgiven! I praise you for the joy that is set before me as I look heavenward. Thank you for the joy your Spirit produces in me. Forgive me for covering up or hiding my joy at times when I should allow it to shine forth. Help me to share this joy with others. I rejoice in you, my Lord, my Redeemer. In the abundant name of Jesus I pray, amen.

Remember: "You have made known to me the paths of life; you will fill me with joy in your presence" (Acts 2:28).

Do: Write out a "happy list"—a list of things you enjoy doing. Now write out a "joy list" naming the reasons you have to rejoice in the

Lord. Compare the two lists. Do they look different from each other? Generally, the things that make you happy are based on temporary enjoyments, while your reasons for joy are based on things that are eternal. Take a moment to thank God for the gift of joy he brings, and ask him to help you open that gift in your daily life.

My Life As a Three-Ring Circus
Enjoying a Life in Balance

I will rejoice in the LORD, I will be joyful in God my Savior. The Sovereign LORD is my strength; he makes my feet like the feet of a deer, he enables me to go on the heights.

—Habakkuk 3:18–19

When is the last time you visited the circus? For me, it was about ten years ago when my daughters were preschoolers. Although my girls didn't fully grasp the degree of heroism involved in the incredible feats, the adults in the audience ooh-ed and ahh-ed throughout the entire program. The circus is definitely one of the "greatest shows on earth"! My only complaint that day was that too much was going on at once. While the acrobats flew through the air in ring one, the tigers performed in the center ring, and the human cannonball was sent into flight in the third. I wish I could have concentrated on everything all at once, but my little brain was overwhelmed.

Unfortunately my life is like a three-ring circus most of the time. What about yours? I often feel like a circus clown trying to juggle five different responsibilities at home while jumping through hoops in my work and scurrying around town running errands and taking my kids to activities. But I don't want to be like the clown on stage with a fake smile painted on his face; I want to have a very real smile on mine. Is it possible in the midst of a fast-paced, circuslike life to experience a deep and lasting joy?

In the previous chapter we said that joy is a constant that's not dependent on outward circumstances. Rather, it's an inner strength, contentment, and peace based on our relationship with the Lord. No one can rob us of our joy, even though difficult situations or painful circumstances can seem to cloud its radiance. We may not have control over some of these circumstances. But in many cases, we can make choices. This chapter is all about making the right choices to ensure that we experience the joy of a balanced life.

The Storm Clouds of Overactivity

Cumulus clouds (those large, puffy ones) are actually named from a Latin word that means "heap." Ironically, the heap of activities we tend to pile on our calendars can be the very thing that cloud-covers our joy.

Although we think of "activity overload" as a current cultural problem, it has age-old roots. Marcus Aurelius, the second-century Roman emperor and philosopher, had this to say about busy schedules: "'If thou wouldst know contentment, let thy deeds be few,' said the sage. Better still, limit them strictly to such as are essential, and to such as in a social being reason demands, and as it demands. This brings the contentment that comes of doing a few things and doing them well."[1] Apparently we are not the first generation to experience overloaded schedules! Human beings always have had and always will have twenty-four hours in each day. It's up to us to make wise choices as to how we will fill that time.

When I was a young girl, my family went out to eat every Sunday after church. And every Sunday, my mother gave me the same advice: "Karol, don't put more on your tray than you can eat." I think I could write a book titled, *Life Lessons Learned at Luby's*! My mother's words can apply to activities as well: "Don't put more on your schedule than you can handle." Like Luby's, life can offer a myriad of good opportunities. That's the problem!

We live in a society in which wonderful opportunities are offered to us on a silver platter each day. Hobbies, family time, sports, career, shopping, school, church, volunteer work—from a plethora of possible activities, we must continually decide what to do and what not to do. For mothers, the list is even bigger, because our kids' activities become our activities, too, as we drive them to and from practices and attend performances.

Solomon said in Ecclesiastes 3:1, "There is a time for everything, and a season for every activity under heaven." It's important for us to realize that there is a time and place for everything—and that time may not be right now. We don't have to do everything this year or this season. How do we make wise choices?

A good formula to follow is encompassed in the acronym PDA. If you're up on technology, you know that a PDA is a "personal digital assistant"—a small, hand-held computer that keeps track of schedules, addresses, phone numbers, and so much more. For our purposes, however, PDA stands for "pray, determine, ask." Let's take a look at each of these components.

Pray. When you are confronted with a decision about adding a particular activity or interest to add to your schedule, ask for God's direction. Many times I've found that God will lead me down a certain road or steer me away from a particular situation when I ask for his guidance. He knows my capabilities and he knows the future, so I defer to his leadership first.

Determine. Determine if the activity has value in your life (or the life of your child). Will it build character? Will it help you reach a long-term goal? Will it take an inordinate amount of time away from family?

Does it allow you to use your gifts and talents? Determine the time commitment and duration of the activity. And finally, determine your motive. Are you choosing to take on a responsibility because of pride—because it will put you in the spotlight or bring you accolades? Are you doing it because everyone else is doing it? Are you being directed by selfish ambition? Many times as we pray about these issues, God will help us see more clearly what our motive really is.

Ask. Have you found, as I have, that whenever someone asks you to take on a leadership or volunteer role, the task inevitably takes about twice as much time as you were told it would? To avoid this problem, ask other people who have done this activity about the time commitment it really takes. Ask them to give you a clearer picture of what's really involved. Ask specific questions about time requirements and other expectations. Keep in mind, however, that each of us is wired a little differently; what frazzled one woman may be an easy job for another. A task that is a piece of cake for an organized person may be overwhelming to someone else who is organizationally challenged.

Another little word that is important to remember is "no." Get comfortable saying it! It may seem ironic, but "no" can be one of the most positive words you can have in your vocabulary when it comes to your schedule. Know your limits. Recognize that you will gain much more respect from doing a few things well than from doing a myriad of activities halfheartedly. It's true that we need to be stretched sometimes and take on an added responsibility that requires a step of faith (as we learned in chapter 4), but such a decision must be made with prayer and care. Count the cost and talk to your heavenly Activity Director. If God is the one doing the stretching, you'll grow stronger in the process. If he's not, you're sure to pop like a rubber band!

Cultivate more joy by arranging your life so that more joy will be likely. —Georgia Witkin

The Balance Beam of Life

My daughter Joy (perfect name for this chapter, don't you think?) has been taking gymnastics for over five years. When she first started, she could barely walk across the balance beam without falling off; but as she progressed, she learned to accomplish a cartwheel on the beam. Recently she mastered a back handspring on the beam. I am absolutely amazed whenever I watch her do this feat! After years of practice, she now completes her routine with ease and rarely falls off the beam. She has learned how to balance herself.

We, too, can learn how to balance ourselves—not necessarily on a balance beam, but in our lives and schedules. Just as Joy developed balance through hours of practice, excellent coaching, and a few falls along the way, we can achieve balance in life through maturity, good advice, and experience.

By maturity I mean the years of growth that develop wisdom in us. One of the blessings of aging (yes, there are some benefits) is that it teaches us to take our time, pray, and make wise, seasoned choices for ourselves and our families. As we mature, we develop greater balance. We also become more balanced as we listen to the wise advice of significant, trusted people in our lives. Did you know that in the business world, some people actually make a living as "life coaches" for others, helping their clients develop goals and maintain a balanced perspective? We may not want to hire a life coach, but we can certainly benefit from a little coaching through life by wise friends, family members, and counselors. The people who know us best can help us look at our schedules and commitments and offer insight into how we can achieve a healthy equilibrium.

When it comes to balance, though, experience is often our best teacher. Through our successes and our mistakes, we begin to learn what does and does not work in our lives. Personally, I can look back and recall times when I was overcommitted or engaged in responsibilities that played to my weaknesses instead of my strengths. In each of these cases I learned to make changes, adjust myself, and find the proper balance. Experience has taught me a great deal about when to say "yes" and when to say "no" to additional activities or responsibilities.

The Perfect Balance

What does it take to live a life of balance? We can find the answer by looking at Jesus and the perfect, balanced life he lived. We read in Luke 2:52 that "Jesus grew in wisdom and stature, and in favor with God and men." That statement identifies four areas of growth and development that are necessary for balanced living. We must pursue them intentionally if we want to follow Jesus' example in our own lives. Let's look at them individually.

Wisdom. I know we have covered the topic of wisdom earlier in this book, but here I want to emphasize the importance of wisdom in maintaining a balance in life. It is through wisdom that we make proper decisions about our schedules. Through wisdom we find opportunities to serve and to get involved in the work that God is doing all around us. A wonderful saying is attributed to German poet Wolfgang von Goethe's mother: "How many joys are crushed underfoot because people look up at the sky and disregard what is at their feet."[2] Wisdom gives us eyes to see the joy that's right there waiting be discovered. If we pursue wisdom, we're certain to find joy in the process.

Stature. Stature relates to the physical side of our well-being, which definitely plays an important role in healthy, balanced living. Physical health is closely connected to emotional health; it's much harder to keep our emotions in balance when our bodies are sick or in pain. A regular exercise routine can be an important key to healthy stature. The obvious physical benefits are a trimmer look and stronger muscle tone, but the emotional benefits are just as real as the physical ones. Studies now show that exercise releases endorphins—neurochemicals in the brain that help head off depression, reduce anxiety, and boost energy.

How do you choose the workout or exercise routine that is right for you? It's important to consider your age, your natural physical abilities, and your overall health. With some sports, like swimming or jogging, you may have to start out slowly and build up to a more demanding workout. It is also crucial to consider your own personal enjoyment. If you hate to run, you probably won't be motivated to get out and jog on a regular basis. Walking may be a better choice; it's considered one of the best exercises for women over forty. Remember to consult your doctor before you start any new exercise program.

You may find it helpful to enlist a workout buddy to make the exercise time more enjoyable and to hold you accountable. My husband and I walk each morning together. I must admit there are mornings I don't want to get out of bed, stretch out, and walk for several miles; but knowing that my husband is expecting me to join him helps me get moving. We have a wonderful time talking along the way (actually, I do 85 percent of the talking, but he's a great listener).

Proper nutrition is another important key to functioning at our peak, both mentally and physically. As we choose to eat a healthy diet of whole grains, lean proteins, fruits, and vegetables, we begin to look better and feel better. In his recent book *Food and Love,* Dr. Gary Smalley points to an amazing connection between what we eat and how we relate to other people. Smalley specifically identifies four categories of food that tend to harm our emotional and physical health: white or refined sugar, white or refined flour, hydrogenated oils or animal fat, and chemically laden foods.[3] In our society of abundant fast and processed foods, we need to ask ourselves, "Am I eating healthy? Am I giving my body the energy and nutrition it needs?"

Sleep is also an important factor that impacts our physical and emotional well-being. I know one thing about myself: a tired Karol is not necessarily a nice Karol. Perhaps you've noticed that about yourself too. Yet many of us fill our calendars with all kinds of activities and fail to schedule enough time for proper sleep. Studies show that most adults need eight hours of rest in order to function at their best. Of course, we all know people who seem to require fewer hours; but personally, I can't relate to those who say they can get by on four hours of sleep night after night. We need to give attention to the amount of sound sleep we're getting and adapt our schedules, if necessary, to make sure we're getting enough. And if on occasion we have a short or restless night, the best thing we can do for ourselves is try to catch a late-afternoon power nap to help us make it through the rest of the day. Ultimately, hearty, healthy sleep can be just the catalyst we need for a happier, more energetic life!

Favor with God. The word *favor* reflects a type of grace in a person or on the part of a giver. In Luke 1:30 we read that Mary, the mother of Jesus, found favor with God. Acts 7:46 says that King David enjoyed God's favor. Unlike salvation by grace, which is a free gift from God that cannot be earned, favor is something that can be deserved or gained. Jesus himself tells us how in John 15:10–14:

> "If you obey my commands, you will remain in my love, just as I have obeyed my Father's commands and remain in his love. I have told you this so that my joy may be in you and that your joy may be complete. My command is this: Love each other as I have loved you. Greater love has no one than this, that he lay down his life for his friends. You are my friends if you do what I command."

We experience the favor of God when we walk in obedience to Christ. The result, Scripture says, is great joy. Sin or disobedience to God, on the other hand, is like a dark cloud that covers our joy. Are there any dark clouds in your life? Do you struggle with a gossiping or backbiting tongue, with bitterness or jealousy, with impure thoughts? Take a few moments right now and ask God to reveal areas of sin in your life that you need to confess. Then ask him to help you turn from them. There is sorrow in our sin, but great joy in a life of obedience!

I want to be perfectly clear: Our eternal destiny is not in question; that's sealed from the moment we step out in faith and trust Christ. As Christians we cannot fall out of grace with God. However, we can draw closer to him as a friend and experience his favor and joy as we walk in his ways. With God's favor, our lives are in balance; without his favor, we tend to be off-kilter.

Favor with mankind. How we relate to others certainly has an effect on the balance and joy reflected in our lives. Jesus spoke often about our relationships with one another. In fact, when someone asked him to name the two greatest commandments, Jesus responded, "'Love the Lord your God with all your heart and with all your soul and with all your mind.' This is the first and greatest commandment. And the second is like it: 'Love your neighbor as yourself'" (Matthew 22:37–39). That's "favor with God and men" in a nutshell! The next chapter is devoted entirely to relationships, but I mention them here because we need to recognize their vital role in healthy, balanced living. As Thomas Aquinas said, "There is nothing on this earth more to be prized than true friendship."[4]

Growing in favor with mankind does not imply that we are to become people pleasers, frantically running around trying to make everyone happy. We must distinguish between the thoughtfulness involved in serving others, which is healthy, and the giving in to people's thoughtless demands, which can be unhealthy. Jesus himself said that not everyone is going to be supportive of us. Matthew 5:11–12 records his words: "Blessed are you when people insult you, persecute you and falsely say all kinds of evil against you because of me. Rejoice and be glad, because great is your reward in heaven, for in the same way they persecuted the prophets who were before you."

There you have it! Because we are followers of Christ, people are not always going to like us. We shouldn't be caught off guard by that. The same kinds of people didn't like the prophets down through the ages. But what should our response be? Jesus tells us to rejoice (there's that *joy* word again) because we can look forward to a heavenly reward. Of course, we're not to go around looking for trouble or causing disagreements. But if people choose to dislike us or even persecute us for following Christ, we shouldn't let it get us down. We can still live a peaceful, balanced life, growing in favor with God and man, if we heed Solomon's general life principle: "When a man's ways are pleasing to the LORD, he makes even his enemies live at peace with him" (Proverbs 16:7).

As positive women we need to focus on developing these four areas of a life in balance: wisdom, stature, favor with God, and favor with mankind. All four are important. Think of them as the four legs of a chair; if one is missing, balance is difficult to maintain. If we work on our relationship with God, for example, but neglect our fellow man, we hide God's light to the world. If we pursue wisdom but fail to maintain our physical well-being, our lives lack the energy to share what we have learned. If we focus on our physical beauty to the detriment of the other areas, our existence is shallow and futile. But by growing in these four areas together, our lives will be in healthy balance and God's joy will shine through us, lighting up a darkened world.

Hormonal Storms

I want to mention one other area that can affect a woman's sense of balance and joy. Perhaps you have noticed there are times during a typical month when you get a run in your hose or forget your lipstick, and you think to yourself, *Oh well.* Then there are other times during the month when the same simple annoyances cause you to completely lose your composure with your spouse, your kids, or your coworkers. The difference comes down to that lovely feminine predicament known as *fluctuating hormones.*

We cannot overlook the part that hormones play in our physical and emotional well-being. In her book *Women and Stress,* Jean Lush likens the cycle of a woman's hormones to the cycle of seasons in a year. Here's a brief summary of what she shares at length in her book. Keep in mind that the symptoms may vary somewhat from month to month:

The *spring phase* starts with the blood flow of the menstrual cycle and is dominated by the hormone estrogen. A woman feels bright, positive, outgoing, energetic, and well coordinated during this time. Little threatens her, and her relationship with her husband and kids is delightful.

The *summer phase* can be described as peaceful, happy, affirming, and creative. The woman is able to accomplish much, but she is a little less assertive. Estrogen continues to dominate, and she feels generally pleased with life.

The *midsummer phase* is the short period in which ovulation occurs. The woman feels euphoric, motherly, peaceful, sensual, and integrative. She loves her husband and kids, who can do no wrong. These feelings are influenced by the production of progesterone.

The *fall phase* begins after ovulation, and now the woman begins

Joy is the echo of God's life within us. —Joseph Marmion

157

to slowly lose energy. Slight depression or the doldrums set in, and she becomes less enthusiastic. Her husband and children don't seem quite so lovable, and her confidence is droopy. Hormone fluctuations during this phase play a part in the unpleasant symptoms.

The *winter phase* occurs in the fourth week of the menstrual month. The woman turns into the "winter witch" as she experiences depression, fatigue, outbursts of emotion (she'll cry over anything), outbursts of temper, frustration, loss of self-control, suspicious or irrational thoughts, low self-esteem, and absent-mindedness. The good news is that the menstrual flow is only a few days away at that point, and she can look forward to feeling much better soon![5]

We should never use our hormones as an excuse for rude or unkind behavior. At the same time, we need to understand our monthly cycle in order to understand ourselves better. Basically, we need to be in harmony with our hormones and recognize when they may be a factor in our attitudes and actions. For instance, when I sense I'm in the winter phase, I know it's not the best time to have a discussion with my husband about a sensitive issue. If I'm feeling annoyed by a salesclerk, I ask myself, *Is the problem really with that person, or is it something going on inside of me?* If I'm in the fall or winter phase and I feel overwhelmed with responsibilities, I know I need to put off making major decisions about my schedule until I move into a more confident phase.

Each of us must pay attention to our own cycles and recognize when our hormones may be affecting us. At certain times it may be wise to talk to a doctor about hormone replacement therapy to bring our hormones into balance. If we understand our hormones and stay alert to their regular fluctuations, we can maintain our balance and our joy through all the seasons.

The Beauty of Joy

A balanced life is a joyful life, and a joyful life is a beautiful life. The true beauty of a positive woman is not simply external, but rather the reflection of the fountain of joy overflowing from her heart. It can be seen in the glow in her eyes, the warmth of her smile, and the kindness of her words.

Our culture is obsessed with outward beauty. You and I shouldn't be. Recently a friend e-mailed me the following comforting facts that have been circulating on the Web. I can't vouch for their complete accuracy, but they seem on target to me:

- There are three billion women who don't look like supermodels and only eighty who do.

- The photos of models in magazines are airbrushed because the models are not perfect.

- If Barbie were a real woman, she'd have to walk on all fours due to her proportions.

- The average woman weighs 144 pounds and wears between a size 12 and 14.

- A 1995 study found that three minutes spent looking at a fashion magazine caused 70 percent of women to feel depressed, guilty, and shameful.

- Twenty years ago models weighed 8 percent less than the average woman. Today they weigh 23 percent less.

As positive women, let's put our focus on developing the true beauty I describe in the following poem:

True Beauty

A woman's beauty does not rest
On her chains of gold or designer dress.
Her beauty is that gentle glow
Which from the heart does clearly grow.
Kindness, peace, hope, and love,
These are the jewels from above.
A smile of joy adorns her face
Founded upon God's true grace.

Jesus said, "You are the light of the world. A city on a hill cannot be hidden. Neither do people light a lamp and put it under a bowl. Instead they put it on its stand, and it gives light to everyone in the house" (Matthew 5:14–15). Let's not allow anything—person, circumstance, or hormone—to cloud our joy. Instead, let's make wise choices every day so that God's joy will shine brightly through us to all of the world.

POWER POINT

⚙ **Read:** The story of two joyful women in Luke 1:39–55. What was the source of the joy these women experienced? How did they express their joy? Were the circumstances in their lives perfect? How were these women an encouragement to each other?

♡ **Pray:** Oh wise and wonderful God, how joyful I become whenever I turn my eyes toward you and recognize your loving kindness and grace! Forgive me for the times I've been too busy to enjoy the sweet fellowship that comes from spending time with you. Help me to balance my time and my life wisely and carefully. Make me aware of choices I've made that tend to cover up my joy, and show me how to set things right so that my joy will overflow once again. What an awesome

God you are—for you truly want me to experience joy! Thank you! In Jesus' name, amen.

💡 **Remember:** "I will rejoice in the LORD, I will be joyful in God my Savior. The Sovereign LORD is my strength; he makes my feet like the feet of a deer, he enables me to go on the heights" (Habakkuk 3:18–19).

☺ **Do:** On a blank piece of paper, draw a simple picture of the sky, including a large sun and several big, puffy clouds. On the sun write, "The joy of the Lord." Add several words describing what this phrase means to you. On the clouds list those areas in your life that tend to hide the joy that's inside you. Then pray and ask God to help you diminish these clouds so that his joy can shine through you to others.

Power Principle #5

Becoming
A
Woman
OF
Love

A woman who loves always has success.

—Vicki Baum

Dear friends, let us love one another,
for love comes from God.

—1 John 4:7

Friendships in the Fast Lane
Maintaining Quality Relationships in a Hurried World

I think that God will never send
A gift so precious as a friend.

—Rosalie Carter

My golden retriever, Honey, is a faithful friend. Every time I walk in the door, he runs and greets me with a wagging tail and what seems to be a big smile on his reddish-brown face. He follows me through the house during the day, from the laundry room to the study to the bedroom and, of course, to the kitchen. At night he lies on the floor by my bed as if to say, "Don't worry, I love you and I'm here to protect you." He's hopelessly loyal. He absolutely loves his walks yet is forgiving when I can't take him. Wouldn't it be delightful if people were as easy to get along with as dogs?

The reality is that people-to-people relationships are a little more work. They can be demanding and complex at times. They require patience, love, forgiveness, and even sacrifice from us. Perhaps you are thinking right now, *Maybe I'll forget friendships and just get a dog!* Yes, pets are great, but they can't replace people in importance in our lives. Remember the Garden of Eden? We learned in chapter 1 that it was not good for Adam to be alone; he needed a human companion. We were created to be relational beings. Solomon recognized the significance of relationships when he wrote, "As iron sharpens iron, so one man sharpens another" (Proverbs 27:17). In Ecclesiastes 4:9–10 he reflected further, "Two are better than one, because they have a good return for their work: If one falls down, his friend can help him up. But pity the man who falls and has no one to help him up!"

Jesus affirmed the high priority of loving and relating to others when he said, "This is my command: Love each other" (John 15:17). He modeled this in his life on earth by surrounding himself with a group of disciples whom he taught, encouraged, and loved. When he prayed in the Garden of Gethsemane, anticipating his death on the cross, he specifically asked Peter, James, and John to stay close to him. Even Jesus wanted close friends around when things got tough.

Peter tells us to "love one another deeply, from the heart" (1 Peter 1:22). Paul encourages us to be "devoted to one another in brotherly love" (Romans 12:10). John speaks forthrightly, "We love because he first loved us. If anyone says, 'I love God,' yet hates his brother, he is a liar. For anyone who does not love his brother, whom he has seen, cannot love God, whom he has not seen. And he has given us this command: Whoever loves God must also love his brother" (1 John 4:19–21).

Clearly the Bible places a high priority on how we relate to one another. So why is it that so many of us struggle to maintain deep and abiding relationships?

Cultural Roadblocks on the Friendship Freeway

Part of the problem is that we live in a hurry-up, get-it-now society. Everything is fast, from food to photos to FedEx. Friendships, on the other hand, take time and nurturing to grow.

Not only is our culture programmed for fast, it is also programmed for busy. When someone asks, "So, what do you do?" we proudly rattle off a long list of the activities we're involved in—careers, family responsibilities, community service, hobbies, and interests. "Oh, I spend time working on my relationships" is not a phrase we typically add to the mix.

Dr. Alan Loy McGinnis, in his best-selling book *The Friendship Factor*, writes, "Why is there such a shortage of friendship? One simple reason: We do not devote ourselves sufficiently to it. If our relationships are the most valuable commodity we can own in this world, one would expect that everyone everywhere would assign friendship highest priority. But for many, it does not even figure in their list of goals. They apparently assume that love will 'just happen.'" He goes on to say, "Significant relationships come to those who assign them enough importance to cultivate them."[1]

The question is, how do we make relationships a priority? How do we cultivate friendships? Is it simply a matter of scheduling our time differently? If the key to relationships were as simple as time management, we could take some lessons on how to use a Palm Pilot and get better relationships with a few keystrokes. Right? No, you and I both know people who have great organizational skills yet lack friendships. We know others who are highly disorganized yet manage to maintain meaningful relationships. Scaling back our activities so we have more time for friendships may be a good idea, but it's not the whole answer. We all know people who are involved in few activities but still long for deeper connections with friends.

So what is the key to quality relationships? I believe it goes back to something our grandmothers told us: "If you want to have friends, you must show yourself friendly." To have good friends, we must be good friends.

Seven Qualities of a Good Friend

After years of speaking to women's groups on the topic of friendship, I have discovered a pattern of characteristics that women typically appreciate in other people. Here are the top seven relationship ingredients that have surfaced over the years. I encourage you to consider these qualities in light of your current friendships and, if you are married, in light of your relationship with your spouse. (They're great building blocks for marriage.) These are qualities to internalize in your own life in order to become a better friend. You can also use them as a measure to consider (not judge) potential friendships in the future.

1. Take a genuine interest in others.

Dale Carnegie, author of *How to Win Friends and Influence People,* said, "You can make more friends in two months by becoming interested in other people than you can in two years by trying to get people interested in you."[2] As we listen to others and show an interest in what is important to them, we begin to truly love and understand them. Every person has an invisible sign around his or her neck that reads, "I want to feel important." Everyone has something to offer this world. We need to search for it, find it, and bring it to the surface.

I've found that scheduling an "Others Hour" is a good way to make time to be attentive to others. What is an Others Hour? It's a sixty-minute period we reserve on our schedules each week in order to focus solely on our friends and their needs. I know for me, if something is not on the calendar, it typically doesn't happen. An Others Hour is a time when we can write a note or make a call or deliver a gift or do a favor. It's a time when we can pray for a certain friend in need. Try it. Who knows? You may find your Others Hour multiplies throughout the week!

2. Be a giver, not a taker.

Ask not what your friends can give to you but rather what you can give to your friends. (Sound familiar? Sorry, John, for reworking your quote.) What can we give to others? How about a smile, a hug, a kind word, a listening ear, help with an errand, a prayer, an encouraging note, a meal? We can come up with many things to give others if we are willing to be attentive to their needs. (Hint, hint: To know someone's needs, you must take a genuine interest in the person first.) Giving may take time. It may take us out of our way. But giving and self-sacrifice are part of the definition of love. I like this little poem by John Oxenham:

> Art thou lonely, O my brother?
> Share thy little with another.
> Stretch a hand to one unfriended,
> And thy loneliness is ended.[3]

3. Be loyal.

Loyalty is a rare commodity in today's world, but it's an absolute requirement in true and abiding friendships. When we are loyal to one friend, we prove ourselves worthy of many.

One way we show our loyalty is through our words—or lack thereof. In fact, a key to being loyal is keeping a tight rein on our tongues. If we're loyal, we won't tear a friend down behind her back or share her personal story without her permission. It's easy to gossip or pass judgment; it's much harder to keep silent. I like what Marsh Sinetar said: "When you find yourself judging someone, silently say to yourself, 'They are doing the best they can right now.' Then mentally forgive yourself for judging."[4] As positive women, we need to make sure our tongues are used for good and not evil. We should be builders with our words, not demolishers.

Jealousy, envy, and a range of other negative emotions can keep us from being loyal. But true loyalty overcomes all of them. I think of the beautiful Old Testament story about the friendship between Jonathan and David. Jonathan had reason to be jealous of his friend, David. Jonathan was King Saul's son and in line to succeed his father to the throne, but God anointed David to be the next king instead. At the same time, David easily could have been angry with Jonathan. Jonathan's father, the king, chased David out of the country and tried to kill him. Yet these two men pledged their loyalty in friendship and never wavered from it. Eventually Jonathan saved David's life, and David continued to show his loyalty to his friend by watching out for Jonathan's son.

Jealousy, envy, bitterness, and anger are all sisters in sin and killers of loyalty in relationships. But if we continually take these emotions to God and ask for his help in overcoming them, we can remain loyal to our friends through the thick and thin of life.

4. Be a positive person.

The most consistent comment I hear about what people want in friendships is this: "I want a friend I can laugh with." We all want friends we can enjoy! People who consistently bring us down with their problems and complaints are generally not the ones we want to pal around with for any length of time. Of course, sometimes a friend will go through a difficult time, and we need to be ready and willing to hold a hand and provide a listening ear. But a friend in need is different than a habitual whiner. We want our friendships to be positive and uplifting— and that means we must be positive, uplifting friends ourselves.

It has been said that there are two kinds of people: those who brighten the room when they enter, and those who brighten the room when they leave. Let's make sure we're brightening our friendships with our presence. Positive women demonstrate an attitude and a spirit that sees God at work in all of life and encourages others to see him too. They are generous with praise, with smiles, and with love, remember-

A friend loves at all times. —Proverbs 17:17

ing what Francis Bacon said: "Friendship doubles joys and halves griefs."[5]

5. Appreciate the differences in others.

Variety is the spice of life. I'm so glad that when I walk into an ice cream store, vanilla isn't the only option! I'm glad, too, that God created people with a variety of personalities, talents, and interests. Each one of us is a unique creation. Mixed together we blend to form the body of Christ.

So why is it that, instead of appreciating our differences, we tend to despise them or become jealous of them? Apparently this was as much a challenge in the early church as it is today. Paul wrote in 1 Corinthians 12:18–25:

> But in fact God has arranged the parts in the body, every one of them just as he wanted them to be. If they were all one part, where would the body be? As it is, there are many parts, but one body.
>
> The eye cannot say to the hand, "I don't need you!" And the head cannot say to the feet, "I don't need you!" On the contrary, those parts of the body that seem to be weaker are indispensable, and the parts that we think are less honorable we treat with special honor....But God has combined the members of the body and has given greater honor to the parts that lacked it, so that there should be no division in the body, but that its parts should have equal concern for each other.

Along with a variety of personalities comes a variety of faults. I am the creative type and love to spend hours writing and brainstorming, but I am a little scatterbrained when it comes to details and being on time. Of course I need to work on my faults, but I also need understanding friends who will bear with me (see Colossians 3:13). At the same time, I need to overlook my friends' faults in other areas. An old Turkish proverb states, "Whoever seeks a friend without a fault remains without one."[6] The truth is, we will never find a perfect friend here on this earth (except Jesus). So let's appreciate our differences, both the good and the bad.

6. Build on common interests.

What is it that brings friends together in the first place? There is usually something that draws us to others—a common hobby, a sport, a Bible study, a volunteer project, a children's activity. My friend Karen and I got to know each other as our daughters grew to be friends at school. Our friendship developed as we took our kids to activities together and talked and planned over the phone. We go to the same church, which gives us another common bond. Karen and her husband, Dick, organize many of the mission opportunities at the church, so Curt and I join them occasionally to help feed the homeless. Since our husbands enjoy hunting and golfing together, we build on their common interests as well.

In our busy society, it can be difficult to create times to get together with people. But if we take advantage of the common activities and interests we have with others, we can fit the time for friendship into our schedules. If you and a friend both like to exercise, work out together. If you both like to read, go to the bookstore together to pick out your next selection, grab some coffee, and talk about the last book you read. If your kids are your common interest, consider getting together on a regular basis to pray for them. The point is to allow your common interests to draw you together.

Married couples need to practice this, too. Many couples tend to get focused on (and frustrated with) their differences while overlooking the common interests that brought them together in the first place.

When that happens they need to go back to basics and begin to build again on their common interests, overlooking each other's faults and appreciating the different qualities they bring into the marriage. Marriages seem to be made in heaven when they start, but they most assuredly need to be maintained and continually tended here on earth. Mignon McLaughlin puts it this way, "A successful marriage requires falling in love many times, always with the same person."[7]

7. Be open, honest, and real.

The word *hypocrite* originally described actors on a stage who covered their faces with masks to conceal their real identities. Today the word describes people who pretend to be something they're not. True friendship cannot be built on false images. We must be true to ourselves. We may think we have to present a faultless picture of ourselves to the rest of the world, but why? No one wants to be friends with someone who is perfect! We simply need to be our best selves and allow people to know the real us.

Of course, being open and honest doesn't mean spilling our guts to everyone. As we already know, loyalty is a rare commodity; when we find it, we know we have a friend we can trust—someone with whom we can share openly about our deepest issues and feelings. George Washington offered some wise words about friendship when he said, "Be courteous to all, but intimate with few; and let those few be well tried before you give them your confidence. True friendship is a plant of slow growth and must undergo and withstand the shocks of adversity before it is entitled to the appellation."[8]

Growing Deeper

Have you noticed that there are certain levels of friendships in life? Not every friend is your best friend. Rather, we have what I call different *circles* of friends. Think of three concentric circles (for all you nonmath majors, think of three circles of different sizes, one inside another inside another). The outer circle represents the large pool of acquaintances we have. These are friends that we know, but not well. We may have fifty to 150 acquaintances, depending on our personalities and the kinds of activities we're involved in. In this outer circle, conversations stay pretty much at surface level:

"How are you doing?"

"Okay, I guess. I've been a little tired lately."

"Oh, me too. I hope you get some rest."

"Thanks. Good to see you."

"Yeah, see you later. Bye."

From within our pool of acquaintances comes the next circle of friends, people we would call "good friends." These are kindred spirits with whom we "click." In fact, a good friendship forms from that "Aha" moment when we first realize we have something in common and begin walking in the same direction side by side. That's what the word *companion* actually means—two people walking in the same direction.

With good friends we tend to reveal ourselves on a deeper level. We share opinions, concerns, facts, and interests. We set aside time for good friends, whether that means meeting them for lunch or simply calling them on the phone. We may have five to twenty-five good friends at different times in our lives.

Finally, from within the garden of good friends grows the wonderful flower that is a best friend, a soul mate, a true heart-to-heart companion. These are the people in our inner circle. They're the lifetime friends with whom we can pick up right where we left off, even when we haven't talked for months. Soul mates share not only opinions and beliefs, but hopes and dreams, struggles and challenges. They enrich one another. We can count ourselves fortunate if we have three or four best friends over a lifetime.

Terry Ann is this type of friend to me. We met during our freshman year at Baylor and soon realized that not only did our personalities mesh, but we also had similar family backgrounds. Tat, as I called her, became my dearest college friend. We were roommates for three years at school and were in each other's weddings. Although we don't see each other often now, we still are able to share our hearts whenever we talk because we have a real depth of friendship between us.

Typically this type of inner-circle friendship doesn't happen overnight but rather over time and through much nurturing and growth. Terry Ann and my sweet friend Beth are two of the soul mates God has given me in my life. My husband, Curt, is another one. A spouse should definitely fit into the soul mate category of friendship. Unfortunately in many marriages, partners have relegated one another to the perimeter circle. If you've done this, invite your spouse back to the inner circle and begin applying the seven principles of friendship to your marriage relationship. You'll be glad you did.

How do we develop friendships that move from acquaintance to good friend and perhaps to soul mate? We begin our friendship circles by making relationships a priority. We apply the seven qualities of a good friend to our own lives, and we ask God to direct us to those people with whom we can connect. Is the goal to see who can have the most friends? No. In fact, when it comes to friendship, quality is more important than quantity. It's difficult to juggle a large number of friends and do it well. Proverbs 18:24 reminds us, "A man of many companions may come to ruin." Quality relationships take time, investment, and yes, self-sacrifice—which is why maintaining meaningful relationships may mean having fewer of them.

Difficult People

Unfortunately, some people we meet don't fit easily into even the outer circles of our lives. We all know them: people who are a little hard to get along with, who perhaps agitate us or annoy us in some way. People who seem to drain us of our emotional strength. As long as there are imperfect people in this world, there will be difficult people in our lives. We may see them at work, in the neighborhood, at a Bible study, or at the places we volunteer. They may be family members. What should we do about them? We can't stick our heads in the sand and pretend they're not there. Ignoring them is not necessarily the most loving approach. Instead, we need to have a plan for dealing with the difficult people who cross our paths at various times. Any effective plan will include the following four R's:

1. Release the need to change the person.

Often our energy is zapped by difficult people because we take on the responsibility of changing them ourselves. We need to take a deep breath and realize that unless people want to change, we cannot force change on them. You and I don't have the ability to make drastic changes in the personalities or habits of others. We can help and assist and at certain times confront, but then we must leave the results up to them and to God.

2. Recognize strengths.

Every person on earth has both positive and negative qualities. "Build on the strengths and manage around the weaknesses," my dad always says. We need to look for the good qualities in others and encourage them to nurture and develop those qualities. If we help people devote more time to their positive strengths, possibly some of the negatives will diminish.

3. Require boundaries.

Many times we dread being around difficult people because they tend to steal our time and energy or demand our attention in some way. We need to determine a limit on how much we can do or give, express it, and stick to it. For example, if a coworker continues to take up time with chitchat or gossip, we can say, "I only have five minutes to talk right now, then I need to get back to my project." Or, "I don't feel comfortable talking about Susie or listening to stories about her, so let's avoid that subject." Self-discipline may be needed to stick to the boundaries we set, but limits will make a difficult relationship much more enjoyable in the long run.

4. Reflect on God's love and forgiveness.

Whenever I think about the myriad of times that God has forgiven me, I find it hard to hold something over someone else. We need to continually extend God's love and forgiveness to the difficult people in our lives. That may mean helping someone turn from sin or a destructive lifestyle. It undoubtedly means praying for them and asking God to work in their lives. We may not be able to change someone, but with God all things are possible. Change is his work, not ours; if we do our part to love and forgive, he will take it from there.

Choose Wisely

Certain friends will come and go throughout life. Other friends will be our friends for life. Such is the cycle of acquaintances and friends, and the fact that some friends move in and out of our lives over the years shouldn't discourage us. When it comes to choosing companions and soul mates, however, we should choose wisely, because these are the people who will have the most significant and long-lasting influence on us. Curt and I tell our teenaged daughters to choose their

A good deed is never lost; he who sows courtesy reaps friendship and he who plants kindness gathers love. —St. Basil

friends carefully, because they will become like the people they hang around. Paul recognized this when he told the Corinthians, "Bad company corrupts good character" (1 Corinthians 15:33). Another oft-quoted statement from Volney Streamer goes like this: "We inherit our relatives and our features and may not escape them; but we can select our clothing and our friends, and let us be careful that both fit us."[9]

In my backyard I have several beautiful rosebushes that I enjoy tending. I try to make sure they have adequate water during the hot summer months, add rose food to their soil twice a year, and keep them pruned every week. My love, care, and attention definitely help to nourish them and encourage their growth. But as much as I would like to take all the credit for their beauty, I must admit there are times when I'm not as attentive to my precious plants as I should be. Yet the roses still seem to flourish in spite of me.

In life, friendships are like roses. They need care and attention to grow. They can be nurtured, but they can't be forced. Sometimes they flourish, not because of anything we do, but because there is an invisible hand—the touch of God—at work in the relationship. As positive women, let us tend our friendship gardens with kindness, forgiveness, and love. And let's open our eyes to the friendships all around us that are just waiting to bloom.

POWER POINT

Read: Matthew 27:55–56, 61 and 28:1–10. What circumstances brought the women in this passage together? Describe the grief and the joy they experienced with one another. What level of friendship do you think these women had with one another? How do you think their friendship developed? Can you name a friend in your life who is most like a "Mary" to you?

♡ **Pray:** I praise you, Father, for you are the truest of friends! Not only have you told us how to love in your Word, you've shown us how to love through your Son's example here on earth. Thank you! Help me now to share that kind of love with others and be a reflection of your love in all my relationships. Help me to be a good friend to the people who are precious to me. May all my friendships honor you, my dearest and closest Friend. In Jesus' name, amen.

♀ **Remember:** "Be devoted to one another in brotherly love. Honor one another above yourselves" (Romans 12:10).

☺ **Do:** On a large piece of paper, draw the three concentric circles mentioned in this chapter. In the outer circle write the names of acquaintances currently in your life. (Don't belabor this; just write the names of the ones who come to your mind first. You don't have to list all two hundred of them.) In the next circle write the names of those people you consider good friends. Finally, in the inner circle write the names of your soul mates or best friends.

Using your drawing as a guide, pray for your friends, and pray for your friendships. Ask God to direct you to a person who may eventually move to the next circle. Decide on some deliberate steps you will take to deepen that friendship—for example, make a phone call, write a note, or set a lunch date.

Creative Compassion
Loving Heartily in a Hurting World

*I am a little pencil in the hand of a writing
God who is sending a love letter to the world.*

—Mother Teresa

Over half a century ago, the *Chicago Daily News* reported a fascinating story under the title, "Love Working Miracles for Mentally Ill in Kansas." The article centered on the amazing success rate of the Topeka State Hospital in returning eight of every ten new mentally ill patients to useful and productive lives outside the facility. Observers throughout the country wanted to know, "What's their secret?" In fact, the hospital's success did not come from electroshock therapy, surgery, group counseling, drugs, or any of the conventional treatments for mental disorders. These played a part, but the real secret was contained in a single word: love.

Dr. Karl Menninger of the famed brother/psychiatrist team explained, "The doctor doesn't cure by any specific treatment. You cure by atmosphere, by attitude, by sympathetic understanding on the part of everyone in the hospital." He went on to say, "By our words and deeds at the hospital, we must gently persuade them that society is worth coming back to. There is none of the professional-staff jealousy that poisons so many institutions. Everyone is on the team. The hospital attendants' opinion is as readily considered as a nurse's or social worker's."[1]

It's easy to talk about love or even to say loving words; but as Dr. Menninger discovered, what people really need is to see love in action. Love in action boosts people to greater heights of development and growth than words or good intentions alone. Can you imagine what would happen if positive women everywhere began putting the power of Christ's love into action on a daily basis? We'd make a lasting and positive difference in this world!

What Love Looks Like

What does real love in action look like? Jesus gave us the perfect picture in his story of the Good Samaritan. A legal expert had just questioned Jesus about the great commandment, "Love your neighbor as yourself." "Who is my neighbor?" the expert wanted to know. Jesus responded immediately with this profound illustration:

"A Jewish man was traveling on a trip from Jerusalem to Jericho, and he was attacked by bandits. They stripped him of his clothes and money, beat him up, and left him half dead beside the road.

"By chance a Jewish priest came along; but when he saw the man lying there, he crossed to the other side of the road and passed him by. A Temple assistant walked over and looked at him lying there, but he also passed by on the other side.

"Then a despised Samaritan came along, and when he saw the man, he felt deep pity. Kneeling beside him, the Samaritan soothed his wounds with medicine and bandaged them. Then he put the man on his own donkey and took him to an inn, where he took care of him. The next day he handed the innkeeper two pieces of silver and told him to take care of the man. 'If his bill runs higher

than that,' he said, 'I'll pay the difference the next time I am here.'"
(Luke 10:30–35 NLT)

Truly this Samaritan man showed love in action. The fact that the
Jewish people despised the Samaritan people makes the story even more
profound. True love crosses over the lines of racism or stereotyping. It
stretches beyond the convenient or the comfortable.

Mother Teresa is a twentieth-century example of someone who put
love in action. She founded the Order of the Missionaries of Charity,
and her selfless commitment to serving the poor in Calcutta, India,
saved the lives of nearly eight thousand people. In 1979 she was
awarded the Nobel Peace Prize for her compassion and devotion to the
destitute. She humbly poured out Christ's love to everyone she
touched, believing that acts of love begin in the small things we do for
others. She said, "We can do no great things—only small things with
great love."[2]

Everyday Illustrations

We can learn from Mother Teresa's example as well as her words.
While love in action can mean opening a home for the impoverished in
India or building an orphanage in Guatemala, it can also mean volunteering at a local hospital or helping to organize cans at a local food
bank. It can mean taking a meal to a new mother or tutoring a child at
the elementary school down the street. Each of these actions is important, and each is needed. Every act of love, great or small, noticed or
unnoticed, makes a positive impact in the world. Even if no one sees
the love and kindness we show to others, God sees, and he knows that
we are obeying his command to love our neighbor.

Let me share with you some stories of a few modern-day
"Samaritans." You probably haven't heard of any of these people.
They're not famous, but they're sincere. They lead full and busy

Dear children, let us not love with words or tongue but with actions and in truth. —1 John 3:18

lives, just like you and me. I pray that their stories encourage and inspire you.

Feeding the homeless. Rip Parker rarely misses a day. Every weekday, every weekend, Rip drives his van packed with sandwiches and water to feed the homeless men and women in downtown Dallas. Cheryl Reinhart, a loving mother and nurse practitioner, joyfully serves with Rip once a month. She also volunteers at least once a week at the Dallas Life Foundation (a homeless shelter), helping to give medical exams to the homeless. Cheryl has known her share of heartache; her teenage son was tragically killed in a car accident. Yet she offers help, love, and hope to others, saying, "We are all put on the earth for something beyond ourselves."

... "And if anyone gives even a cup of cold water to one of these little ones because he is my disciple, I tell you the truth, he will certainly not lose his reward" (Matthew 10:42).

Adopting girls. Lance and Carol Wagers realized their life was in for a change, but they didn't realize how big the change would be. In their early fifties and after twenty-nine years of running a huge cheerleading company, they felt God call them into semiretirement. Since they had no children, they felt their life was an open book, and they were excited to see what story God would write on the rest of their lives.

On a mission trip down the Amazon River in Brazil, they encountered a poor family with nine children. Before they left the family's village, the mother came to Lance and Carol and asked if they would take her two youngest daughters back to the United States with them. She had been praying for years for a Christian family to adopt her daughters, then ten and eleven years old. She wanted the girls to get away from their difficult environment and have an opportunity for a better life. Hearing very clearly God's call to them, the Wagers obeyed. They eventually adopted Leni and Loraine and became an instant family with teenagers.

... *"Religion that God our Father accepts as pure and faultless is this: to look after orphans and widows in their distress and to keep oneself from being polluted by the world"* *(James 1:27).*

Visiting those in prison. "Nothing can prepare you perfectly for ministry to death row inmates," says army major Kathryn Cox. Kathryn has been ministering to inmates on "The Row" and their families since 1986. While her undergraduate degrees in psychology and journalism and her master's degree in criminal justice are helpful as she coordinates Bible correspondence courses for thirty thousand inmates through the army's Texas division, she believes God developed a strong spirit of compassion and understanding in her for this special ministry. She says that everything she has witnessed through her ministry "attests mightily to a salvation that can penetrate any locked door."[3]

... *"Come, you who are blessed by my Father; take your inheritance, the kingdom prepared for you since the creation of the world. For I was hungry and you gave me something to eat, I was thirsty and you gave me something to drink, I was a stranger and you invited me in, I needed clothes and you clothed me, I was sick and you looked after me, I was in prison and you came to visit me"* *(Matthew 25:34–36).*

Reaching children with HIV. Beth Dykhuizen loves children. As the mother of four, she is devoted to serving her family and raising her kids to be fine Christian young people. Early on, Beth learned how painful it is to see innocent children suffer. Her own son, Kurt, was born with Goldenhar Syndrome, which meant he had numerous birth defects and required over eighteen surgeries. Watching her son go through these physical challenges drew Beth's heart to other hurting children.

"People used to tell me that I am very sensitive to other people's needs," Beth says. "But it made me think, what am I doing with it? I finally realized that the sensitivity was not beneficial unless I acted upon it. When I would see suffering in this world, I would question why God would allow it. But then I realized that God had made me to reach out, touch the suffering, and show them his love."

As a member of her church's missions committee, Beth sought out ministries in need of volunteers and came across an organization that helps children and their families impacted by HIV. Beth knew immediately that this was where she wanted to serve. She started taking care of the babies—loving them, feeding them, and changing their diapers. Her daughter Connie began to help too. Because her own son had such loving support at her home, her heart went out to those children who did not have such comfort.

... *"I tell you the truth, whatever you did for one of the least of these brothers of mine, you did for me" (Matthew 25:40).*

Teaching generations. Jan Gilliland earned her masters of divinity from Southwestern Baptist Theological Seminary at a time when few women pursued advanced degrees. She planned to go away to the mission field but found her mission was in her own home. Having successfully raised four children, she now pours her talents into the lives of her grandchildren and the community around her. Every summer she organizes a Cuzzins Camp for her grandchildren who are five years of age and up. The camp creatively centers on a different biblical theme each year, giving Jan the opportunity to pour God's Word into generation after generation. Her daughter Leslie says this about her: "Mom is always doing something for someone else. I remember hitting the 'sophomore slump' at Baylor. She listened patiently and then asked me, 'What are you doing for other people?' That truly is the theme of her life."

... *"Do nothing out of selfish ambition or vain conceit, but in humility consider others better than yourselves. Each of you should look not only to your own interests, but also to the interests of others" (Philippians 2:3–4).*

Showing mercy to many. Probably one of the most compassionate people I know is Karen McFarland. Her life is a picture of devotion to

God and commitment to serve others with his love. A wonderful mother, she serves at her kids' school. She faithfully feeds the homeless once a month. She organizes mission opportunities at our church, so that many willing hearts can reach out to the community in Christ's love. She opens her home for friends, family, meetings, and gatherings. Karen also cares for her elderly mother-in-law, who lives in a retirement community nearby. Karen is a blessing to others not only for her acts of kindness, but also for her mind of mercy that is always thinking of others.

…*"Let this mind be in you which was also in Christ Jesus, who, being in the form of God, did not consider it robbery to be equal with God, but made Himself of no reputation, taking the form of a bondservant, and coming in the likeness of men" (Philippians 2:5–7 NKJV).*

God has a gift he wants to give to the world through each of us, and that gift is love. But as we can see from these examples, love has many faces. It displays itself uniquely in and through each individual life. Colossians 3:12 tells us, "Since God chose you to be the holy people whom he loves, you must clothe yourselves with tenderhearted mercy, kindness, humility, gentleness, and patience" (NLT). The form each of these pieces of God's wardrobe takes will be different on different individuals. But one thing is constant: When we clothe ourselves with these things, God's love becomes visible to everyone around us.

The Law of Kindness

Have you noticed that some people seem to have a gift for loving others? Romans 12:6–8 tells us that God has given each of us gifts in certain areas. "Service" and "kindness" are two of the gifts in the list. Obviously, many of the women mentioned in this chapter have gifts of service or kindness. Other women may have different gifts such as teaching or administration or encouragement. But even when kindness is not our predominant gift, it still should be a quality that is evident in our lives. Love and kindness are two of the fruits of the work of the Holy Spirit (see Galatians 5:22–23). Love should always be a central theme in the life of a follower of Christ.

First John 4:7–8 says, "Dear friends, let us love one another, for love comes from God. Everyone who loves has been born of God and knows God. Whoever does not love does not know God, because God is love." Christians ought to be the most loving people in the world. Unfortunately, that's not always the case. From backbiting to gossip to harassing people who don't know Christ, our negative behavior can speak volumes. But when the people around us experience true kindness and love through the Holy Spirit at work in us, they begin to get a picture of Christ's abiding love. According to Proverbs 31:26, a positive woman exhibits the "law of kindness with her tongue" (NKJV). Could others say that about us? Do kindness and love control our words and actions?

Of course, love is not always warm and fuzzy. Sometimes love means encouraging someone to become a better person. At times the most compassionate thing we can do is to confront a friend or loved one and then offer a step up—a lift to help the person move forward in a positive direction. In such cases, kindness should be coupled with wisdom as we speak the truth in love.

A friend of mine (I'll call her Susan) uses the following formula for encouraging people to experience health and wholeness when they've been caught in a destructive lifestyle. She actually formulated these principles when her daughter's friend began to make unwise relationship choices and needed direction and help. Susan told her daughter to talk to her friend and follow these three steps:

1. *Revelation.* Say, "Here's what you are doing." In this case, Susan's daughter helped her friend recognize her destructive behavior.

2. *Reaction.* Say, "Here's what could happen." The daughter pointed out the consequences of her friend's behavior.

3. *Road to success.* Say, "Here's a better way." The daughter offered tips on how to be a positive friend.

Susan will be the first to tell you that these principles must be delivered in kindness and love. Furthermore, we'd be wise to remember that advice is best offered when it is requested or desired; otherwise we may be wasting our time. As we learned in the last chapter, any change, reaction, or result is in God's hands; our responsibility is simply to love.

Jesus is our example when it comes to "speaking the truth in love" (Ephesians 4:15) and helping others choose a more positive direction in life. He showed us love by showing us a better way. In his Sermon on the Mount, he gave us a loving and beautiful picture of how to enjoy a happy life. The word *blessed* in this passage comes from the same Greek root (*makarios*) as the word *happy*:

Blessed are the poor in spirit, for theirs is the kingdom of heaven.

Blessed are those who mourn, for they will be comforted.

Blessed are the meek, for they will inherit the earth.

Blessed are those who hunger and thirst for righteousness, for they will be filled.

Blessed are the merciful, for they will be shown mercy.

Blessed are the pure in heart, for they will see God.

Blessed are the peacemakers, for they will be called sons of God.

Blessed are those who are persecuted because of righteousness, for theirs is the kingdom of heaven. (Matthew 5:3–10)

Compassion is a feeling of sorrow for the sufferings or troubles of others, along with an urge to help. Jesus showed his love and compassion toward us by encouraging us to leave behind our dark, empty lives and experience a life that's abundant, happy, and blessed. Because God loves us, he taught us how to live!

Taking Action

In God's vocabulary, love is an action word. Paul describes true love in 1 Corinthians 13:4–7: "Love is patient, love is kind. It does not envy, it does not boast, it is not proud. It is not rude, it is not self-seeking, it is not easily angered, it keeps no record of wrongs. Love does not delight in evil but rejoices with the truth. It always protects, always trusts, always hopes, always perseveres."

You and I can't deliver this kind of love in our own strength. But if we allow ourselves to be open vessels in God's hands, God's love can pour through us to others. John reminds us, "This is how we know what love is: Jesus Christ laid down his life for us. And we ought to lay down our lives for our brothers" (1 John 3:16). God demonstrated his own great love for us in that while we were still sinful people, he sent his Son, Jesus, to die for us (see Romans 5:8). Now we can love too—because the God of love lives inside of us.

Several years ago I began collecting golf hats from the various cities and restaurants our family visits on vacations. One of my favorites is from the Hard Rock Café. It's black and white, and it sports a simple logo on the back that says, "Love all; serve all." What a great motto! As positive women, we should wear that motto continually on our hearts and minds every day. Jesus showed us what it means to love all and serve all. May this be our creed as we shine brightly in our world for him!

POWER POINT

⚙ **Read:** The story of Dorcas (also known as Tabitha) in Acts 9:36–43. What was Dorcas known for in her community? Why was there such an outpouring of grief when she died? What great miracle occurred in this story, and how did it affect others? Do you know someone who is like Dorcas?

♡ **Pray:** Oh, compassionate heavenly Father, may my life be a reflection of your love! I know that I am able to love only because you have loved me so abundantly. Help me now to love others as you have loved me. I thank you that your love is complete in kindness, compassion, service, and truth. May it overflow to all the people in my life! Help me to be a vessel you can use to show your love and compassion to the world. In Christ's loving name, amen.

💡 **Remember:** "Finally, all of you, live in harmony with one another; be sympathetic, love as brothers, be compassionate and humble" (1 Peter 3:8).

☺ **Do:** Pray and ask God to direct you to one area of service or ministry through which you can show his love to others. It may be something you do once a week, once a month, or sporadically throughout the year. Ask God to open up an opportunity that will best utilize your unique gifts and talents. Then decide today to actively pursue that opportunity to show his compassion to the people around you.

Power Principle #6

Becoming A Woman of Courage

Courage is not simply one of the virtues,
but the form of every virtue at the testing point.

—C. S. Lewis

Have I not commanded you? Be strong and courageous.
Do not be terrified; do not be discouraged,
*for the L*ORD *your God will be with you wherever you go.*

—Joshua 1:9

High Heels on a Dirt Road
Walking with Courage down the Road of Life

*Leadership is capitalizing on a God-given window of opportunity
when it is presented. Not tepidly. Not timidly. But boldly, by jumping
into the fray with both feet and a determination to change your world
with your ideas and your proposals.*

—Michelle Easton

In 1998 Michelle Toholsky felt that God was leading her to create a quality fashion magazine with a Christian emphasis. She launched out on this monumental project with little capital but loads of courage. If God was guiding her to do this magazine, she figured, he would provide a way. She didn't know important people; she didn't have the background, knowledge, or experience to create this magazine; she simply knew God was with her and leading her. Michelle says she grew up in a family that exhibited this type of courage based on their faith in God.

"When you truly believe God has no limits, you have the courage to move forward," says Michelle. "It's when we get our eyes on our circumstances and our own limitations that we begin to sink, as Peter did when he was walking on the water."

The first issue of *Shine* magazine leaped off the presses in 1999. Sheila Walsh graced the cover, the photographer worked at his own cost, and the writers contributed articles without compensation. There were fifty subscribers, and the printer agreed to print 150 issues to distribute to bookstores around the nation.

Michelle experienced struggles along the way, but God always provided the funds for her to keep going. By January 2002 *Shine* had reached a distribution of 60,000, and the numbers keep growing.

"If we wait until things are perfect, we will never accomplish anything," Michelle told me. "For me, stepping out in courage meant stepping into God's work. I wasn't afraid of failing, because I knew if I fell, I would fall right into his arms."

Michelle Toholsky is a picture of a woman of courage—courage coupled with faith in a God who is bigger than any circumstance. The road she took wasn't easy; it had its twists, turns, and potholes. But her courage and faith saw her through.

As Michelle discovered, faith in an all-powerful God goes hand in hand with courage. When we choose to move courageously ahead, we are actually putting our faith into action. It was courageous faith that led David to fight Goliath when no one else would step up to the plate. It was courageous faith that inspired Joan of Arc to lead French troops into battle, thus turning the tide of the Hundred Years War. Courageous faith motivated Harriet Tubman to lead Southern slaves to freedom through the Underground Railroad. Courageous faith inspired Corrie Ten Boom to hide Jewish people in her home during World War II; after she was caught, it helped her survive life in a Nazi death camp.

Courage takes us out of our comfort zones and into magnificent places we could never reach on our own. When we step out in faith, we choose to depend on God—and not ourselves—for both direction and strength for the journey. Over and over in the Old Testament, God told his people, "Be strong and of good courage," as he led them forward to the Promised Land. "Oh, love the Lord, all of you who are his people," the psalmist wrote, "for the Lord protects those who are loyal to him,

Those who hope in the LORD will renew their strength. They will soar on wings like eagles; they will run and not grow weary, they will walk and not be faint. —Isaiah 40:31

but harshly punishes all who haughtily reject him. So cheer up! Take courage if you are depending on the Lord" (Psalm 31:23–24 TLB).

Taking a Step of Courage

One of my favorite Bible stories is the epic tale of Deborah found in the fourth chapter of the Book of Judges. She was a true hero—the only woman named in the Bible who was placed in high political leadership by the consent of the people. She served the Israelites in many ways, first as a counselor, then as a judge, and finally as their leader in battle. How did she rise to such prominence in a male-dominated society? Through her faith. She trusted God implicitly, and through this trust, courage was born.

At the time this story begins, the Israelites had been cruelly oppressed by the pagan king of Canaan for twenty years. Now they cried out to God for help. Deborah, who was holding court under a palm tree and advising people in disputed matters, heard this cry and sent for a man named Barak. She relayed a message from God: Barak was to take ten thousand men with him to Mount Tabor. When they arrived, God would lure Sisera, the commander of the Canaanite troops, along with his men and nine hundred iron chariots, to the Kishon River. There Barak would easily defeat them.

Barak's response to Deborah was slightly wimpy: "If you go with me, I will go; but if you don't go with me, I won't go" (Judges 4:8).

So Deborah agreed to go to the battlefield. "But because of the way you are going about this," she told Barak, "the honor will not be yours, for the LORD will hand Sisera over to a woman" (v. 9).

Sure enough, when the Israelites reached Mount Tabor, Sisera gathered his army and chariots at the Kishon River. Deborah told Barak, "Go! This is the day the LORD has given Sisera into your hands. Has

197

not the LORD gone ahead of you?" (v. 14). So Barak advanced, and with the Lord's help, the Israelites easily routed Sisera and his army.

"Has not the Lord gone ahead of you?" What a profound statement by a courageous woman of faith! Deborah didn't focus on the nine hundred iron chariots (which had the Israelites shaking in their boots); she saw a powerful God who had directed them to move forward.

Is God directing you to move forward? What enemies are hindering you—fear, doubt, worry? Like Deborah, be strong and of good courage. Has not the Lord gone ahead of you? Is he not able to do all things? If he is guiding you, he will provide for you!

Against the Odds

Courage can take many forms. Think of Marie Curie (you read her story briefly in chapter 1), who wrote in her journal, "I felt the impossibility of going on." She penned these words on the day her husband, who was also her coworker, died in a tragic accident involving a horse-drawn wagon. Yet Marie *did* go on to achieve great advancements in the study of uranium. Think of Rosa Parks, who courageously stayed in her seat on a bus rather than relinquishing it to a white man, thus making an historical breakthrough against social injustice. Think of Wilma Rudolph, who, after a series of childhood illnesses, lost the use of her left leg. Doctors told her she would never walk, but Wilma courageously pushed beyond her limitations and learned not only to walk but to run. She became the first American woman to win three gold medals in track and field in a single Olympiad.[1]

A woman's courage is displayed when she must face great odds—whether she chooses the circumstances or they choose her. My friend Leslie didn't choose the challenges she has faced in the past two years of her life. After an accident in which their car rolled over and was totaled, Leslie and her daughter Amanda suffered minor injuries. Not long after that, Leslie's mother went into the hospital with intestinal problems and passed away after several weeks of complications. Just recently Leslie's other daughter, Natalie, was rushed to the hospital in critical condition after a go-cart accident. Because of severe liver damage, Natalie spent a week in the hospital followed by a long period of recovery at home. Suffice it to say, Leslie and her husband, Roger, have grown tremendously in courage and strength over this period.

Where did they find the courage to face each new challenge? Leslie and Roger will tell you they didn't feel particularly courageous ahead of time; rather, the courage to go on arrived just at their moment of need. They say it came from the Lord—and from the people he brought to their side to encourage and help them. It came from the knowledge that their loving, all-wise God was with them and would be with them, whatever happened.

That's where our courage as Christians comes from. We know that no matter how a situation turns out, God will be there to help us and see us through. What did Jesus say to his disciples when he told them to go out and change the world with the gospel message? "And surely I am with you always, to the very end of the age" (Matthew 28:20).

My dad has always said, "The greatest motivational statement ever uttered is, 'God is with you.'" Not that we have a guarantee of success or a guarantee that everything will turn out the way we want it to; no, we simply have a guarantee that God is with us.

In Deuteronomy 31:6 we read these words of Moses, spoken to the Israelites as they progressed toward the Promised Land: "Be strong and courageous. Do not be afraid or terrified because of them [the enemy armies], for the LORD your God goes with you: he will never leave you nor forsake you." Let's take hold of that message for today. The Lord our God goes with us. He will not leave us or forsake us. Take courage!

"Let's Roll"

Todd Beamer was one of the passengers aboard United Flight 93 on September 11, 2001. As the people on the flight became increasingly aware of the fate the terrorists had planned for them, Todd and some of the others made a plan to fight back. After quietly praying the Lord's Prayer with a telephone operator and passing on a message to his family that he loved them, he dropped his cell phone and said, "Let's roll." Along with several other passengers, Todd bravely overpowered the hijackers, and the plane ended up crashing in an empty field in Pennsylvania rather than into a crowded building in Washington, D.C. Todd and the others gave their lives to save many more.

Afterward, Lisa Beamer, Todd's widow, chose courage instead of defeat in response to the news of her husband's death. Seven months pregnant, Lisa left her hometown of Cranbury, New Jersey, and boarded the same flight from Newark to San Francisco that her husband had taken six weeks earlier. In doing so, she set an example of strength and courage for an entire grieving nation. The trip was not only symbolic but purposeful. She met with Todd's former business associates and launched the Todd M. Beamer Foundation, an organization intended to provide health insurance, mental health support, and financial-planning services for the twenty-two children who lost parents on Flight 93.

On November 10, 2001, Lisa addressed twenty thousand women gathered at a Women of Faith conference in Philadelphia. She said, "If my choice is to live in fear or to live in hope, I've chosen to live in hope."[2] Recently she gave birth to a healthy baby girl—even as her story of courage continues to give birth to strength and hope in the hearts of those who hear it. Who can know the countless lives that Lisa and Todd Beamer have touched through their separate examples of courage?

The Courage to Stand for What Is Right

There are many stories of courage throughout American history—courage in times of war, courage during natural disasters, and courage in standing up for convictions. Susan B. Anthony's life is one example. Susan was born in 1820. When she was eighteen years old, she took a job as a teacher to help alleviate her family's desperate financial situation. For fifteen years she taught in both public and private schools, never making more than three dollars a week (with one of those dollars going for boarding). When she discovered that male teachers made three times what she did, she became concerned about the inequalities in men's and women's salaries.

That concern went on the back burner when Susan decided to devote her time and energy to the temperance movement. Before long she became discouraged by the limited role women were allowed to have in the established movement, however, so she helped start the Woman's State Temperance Society in New York. From 1856 to 1861, Susan turned her attention to the antislavery movement before finally picking up the cause that had originally caught her attention. She committed her later years to the women's suffrage movement, helping to organize the National Woman's Suffrage Alliance in 1904.

Susan's road was not easy. She endured physical discomfort, name-calling, and disrespect, but she courageously pressed on for what she believed was right. It took courage and conviction for her to stand up for her belief in the equality of women before God. She always remembered the words of her precious Quaker father: "Tolerate not evil against humanity. And when thee is powerless to do anything else, speak with vigor."[3] Certainly Susan lived up to her father's words.

There are times when we must have the courage to stand up for our

My job is to take care of the possible and trust God with the impossible. —Ruth Bell Graham

convictions, even when very few are standing with us. Some of us are called to be active and speak out like Susan B. Anthony, while others are called to quietly hold strong like Rosa Parks. Whenever and however we take a stand, we must do it prayerfully and with wisdom. And we must do it with love and kindness, as we discussed in the last chapter.

When my daughters were in their early years of grade school, they were invited to join a girls organization that was quite popular not only in our school but around the nation. I was hesitant, however. I'd read not long before that the organization had started to veer away from some of the standards our family valued. Several other mothers had the same concern, I soon discovered.

Instead of fighting the established national organization, a few of us decided to start our own after-school club for girls. We named it "Sonshine Girls." The meetings would teach character and values in a clublike environment, using biblical standards as the guide. Each month the girls would go on a field trip to put into action the character quality they'd learned. Well, Sonshine Girls took us all by storm. We had sixty-four girls at the first meeting! The idea spread, and today Sonshine Girls can be found in schools and homeschool groups around the nation.

It took courage to start. We were beginning from scratch with no curriculum, no funds, and no assurance of support. We were also going against the grain of the established organization, and that rubbed some powerful women the wrong way. We were called divisive and self-righteous, even though we were only following our convictions in a creative and loving way.

Quite honestly, I was both surprised and hurt by many of the reactions we received. There were times when I felt discouraged and fearful about moving forward with Sonshine Girls. The task seemed overwhelming—and I didn't like the opposition. I wanted to quit. Then one day I opened my Bible, searching for encouragement. My eyes fell immediately on Joshua 1:9: "Be strong and of good courage; do not be afraid, nor be dismayed, for the LORD your God is with you wherever you go" (NKJV).

This passage filled me with such hope and courage that I immediately called my Sonshine Girl coworker and shared it with her. With great excitement she told me that God had just led her to Deuteronomy 31:6, which says nearly the same thing: "Be strong and courageous. Do not be afraid or terrified…for the LORD your God goes with you." Amazing! God gave both of us this same message from his Word to remind us to stand tall. He was saying to us, "Don't be afraid to do what I have put in your heart to do. I'm in this with you." Because we continued to go forward with courage, many girls (and their moms) have now been blessed through Sonshine Girls.

My Help Comes from the Lord

Do you feel courageous? Neither do I! The truth is, we may not know we have the courage to face a challenge until that challenge comes. In ourselves we are weak; we are clothed in human frailties. But God promises us that when we are weak, *he* is strong. Courage is his work in us. Paul said this about one of his own challenges:

> Three times I pleaded with the Lord to take it away from me. But he said to me, "My grace is sufficient for you, for my power is made perfect in weakness." Therefore I will boast all the more gladly about my weaknesses, so that Christ's power may rest on me. That is why, for Christ's sake, I delight in weaknesses, in insults, in hardships, in persecutions, in difficulties. For when I am weak, then I am strong. (2 Corinthians 12:8–10)

Like Paul, you and I are weak. But also like Paul, we can find our strength, our courage, and our help in the Lord. Whatever circumstances we face, we don't have to despair. God is sufficient to see us through all the challenges at hand.

Anne Peters is a talented poet and a dear Christian. God has done a miraculous work in her life, bringing her through a childhood filled with struggle and abuse. Today she is a positive woman—and a courageous one. Our chapter closes with one of her many poems about courage.

If Courage Could Be Mine

I asked you one day Father
If courage could be mine
You told me to be patient
All virtues come with time.

I looked for her in trials
I looked for her in pain
For it was hard to see her
When comfort came again.

Never did I notice
Until the years went by
That courage had been watching
When tears did cloud my eyes.

She came upon a whisper
And held my hand in hers
Slowly she did lift me
To take away my fears.

She woke my heart up slowly
Or I would turn away

Too frightened by the picture
Of the love God gave away.

I felt my spirit growing
No fear or shadows fell
Courage was beneath me
My faith the deepest well.

I asked you one day Father
If courage could be mine
You said that it was with me
And had been for all time.

POWER POINT

Read: Judges 4 and 5, the story of two brave women and a song of praise. What evidence do you have that Deborah's courage was based on her faith in God? Although she was a courageous leader and hero, to whom did she give honor? Think back to a time in your life when you demonstrated courage. Where did your courage come from, and who received the credit?

Pray: Lord, you are my rock and my refuge. You are a very present help in time of need. Thank you for promising that you will never leave me nor forsake me. Thank you that although I may not always understand your ways, I can always depend on your faithfulness. You are worthy of my trust. Help me to have the courage to boldly step out in faith, following your direction. May my life, my actions, and my courage ultimately bring glory to you. In Jesus' name, amen.

Remember: "Be strong and courageous. Do not be afraid or terrified because of them, for the LORD your God goes with you; he will never leave you nor forsake you" (Deuteronomy 31:6).

☺ **Do:** Think of one or two people you know (or know about) who need courage right now. Pray for them, asking that they would feel God's presence and strength. When you're done, write a letter of encouragement to let them know you are praying for them.

Next, think of an area in your own life in which you need courage. Take your concern before the Lord in prayer. Ask him to strengthen your heart and sear into your memory the greatest motivational statement of all time: "God is with you."

Facing Fears
Finding the Courage to Move Forward

Courage is not the absence of fear;
rather it is the ability to take action in the face of fear.

—Nancy Anderson

My friend Pam came over to my house recently for our regular prayer time. Usually a group of five moms, all with teenage daughters, meet together every Wednesday to pray. On this particular Wednesday, however, Pam and I were the only ones who could make it, so we began talking about the fact that both of us have daughters who are about to get their driver's licenses. Pam's voice became serious as she told me that a family she knew had just been through the grievous loss of one of their daughters in a car accident. Instantly I felt a surge of fear pump through my body. *How will Grace survive in the brutal Dallas traffic?* I thought. *What if she doesn't see a stop sign? What if she looks away for just a moment to adjust the radio?* Anything is possible, Pam and I agreed. We both stared at each other with fear in our eyes.

What could we do to protect our sweet daughters? Keep them from driving until they turned thirty-five? Bar all other traffic from the highways so that only our daughters could drive on them? As much as Pam and I liked these options, we knew they weren't realistic. There was really only one thing we could do: face our fears, move forward, and pray for God's protection over our loved ones.

Fear tends to grip all of us in different areas and at different times in our lives. When we allow it to get the upper hand, it captures us in its net and keeps us from experiencing the abundant and fulfilling life God intends for us. "Where fear is," the philosopher Seneca said, "happiness is not."[1]

The story is told of an old farmer who was sitting on the steps of his rickety shack when a stranger approached. Trying to initiate conversation, the stranger asked, "How's your wheat coming along?"

"Didn't plant none," the farmer replied.

"Really?" said the stranger. "I thought this was good wheat country."

"I was afraid it would rain," the farmer said.

"How is your corn crop?" the stranger persisted.

"Ain't got none. Afraid of corn blight."

"Well, sir, how are your potatoes?"

"Didn't plant no potatoes either. Afraid of the potato bugs."

"Well, then, what in the world did you plant?" the exasperated stranger asked.

"Nothin'," said the farmer. "I just played it safe."[2]

Oh, the stifling effect fear can have on our lives! The farmer's story reminds me of the parable Jesus told about the wealthy man who entrusted his servants with the care of his property when he went away on a journey. To one servant he gave five talents (a talent was a measure of money in Jesus' day); to another servant he gave two talents, and to another, one. The servant with five talents went out immediately and put his master's money to work earning five more talents. The servant with two talents also gained two more. But the servant with one talent dug a hole in the ground and hid his money.

When the master returned, he was pleased with the two servants who had invested their talents wisely. He said to each of them, "Well done, good and faithful servant! You have been faithful with a few things; I will put you in charge of many things. Come and share your master's happiness!" (Matthew 25:21, 23). But the third servant didn't receive such a high compliment:

> "Then the man who had received the one talent came. 'Master,' he said, 'I knew that you are a hard man, harvesting where you have not sown and gathering where you have not scattered seed. So I was afraid and went out and hid your talent in the ground. See, here is what belongs to you.'
>
> "His master replied, 'You wicked, lazy servant!…Take the talent from him and give it to the one who has the ten talents. For everyone who has will be given more, and he will have an abundance. Whoever does not have, even what he has will be taken from him.'" (Matthew 25:24–29)

Why did the third servant hide his talent? He said it himself: "I was afraid." You see, fear paralyzes us. It keeps us from moving forward in life and making full use of the gifts and talents God has given us. In my line of work, I meet many potential authors. Some are talented writers, but they do not submit their work to publishers because they are afraid of rejection. Fear keeps them from taking that next step forward.

Jesus told us plainly that we should let our lights shine, not cover them under a basket or bushel (see Matthew 5:14–16). Yet like the third servant, we often hide our talents because that's the safe and comfortable thing to do. And in the process, we miss out on hearing God say, "Well done, good and faithful servant." As positive women, we need to throw off those baskets! We need to face our fears, move ahead, and let our lights shine brightly for Christ in this dark world.

Fear Not!

God does not want us to live our lives in fear. As part of my research for this chapter, I decided to find out how many times the phrase, "Fear not," is proclaimed by God in the Old and New Testaments. Pulling out my analytical concordance of the Bible, I started counting, but the task quickly proved quite daunting. While I was still in the early books of the Old Testament, I decided to stop and pay one of my research assistants (my daughter Grace who needs to earn gas money for the car) to count the rest for me. She came up with approximately seventy-five.

As that number attests, God frequently and continually comforted his people with the words, "Fear not." They're the words God said to Abraham as he began his journey of faith to the Promised Land. They're the words the angel used when he visited Mary and declared she would be the mother of the Son of God. And they're the words spoken by God and his messengers to many other people in between.

Today God is saying these very same words to you and me. Romans 8:15 says, "For you did not receive a spirit that makes you a slave again to fear, but you received the Spirit of sonship. And by him we cry, '*Abba,* Father.'" Hebrews 13:6 adds, "So we say with confidence, 'The Lord is my helper; I will not be afraid. What can man do to me?'"

The only thing the Bible tells us to fear is God himself. This is not the shaking-in-your-boots, panicky, trembling kind of fear, but rather a reverence, awe, and respect for who God is and what he can do. It's a healthy fear—the kind of fear we talked about in chapter 5 when we said, "The fear of the Lord is the beginning of wisdom." Only as we fear God in this reverential way can we walk in wisdom and confidence throughout our lives.

But fear—the unhealthy kind—can be subtle. Often it creeps into our hearts undetected, quietly sets up camp, and then slowly immobilizes us in a certain area. We don't know we've been infiltrated until we suddenly realize we can't move forward in a particular part of our lives. Facing that fear is like waging war against an entrenched enemy. Victory is possible, however, if we follow this four-part battle plan:

1. Recognize the enemy.

In any type of warfare, the first step is to identify the enemy. Theologian A. W. Tozer said, "Fear is of the flesh and panic is of the devil."[3] We know from 2 Timothy 1:7 that fear is not from God. Rather, it is from Satan, who uses it as a weapon to "steal and kill and destroy" our faith, our joy, and our effectiveness as Christians (John 10:10).

Some fears grip our entire being; others give us only a twinge of worry now and then. However they manifest, they need to be identified specifically. Ask God to reveal areas in your life where fear has sneaked in and made a home for itself. Are you afraid for your family's safety? Are you afraid your spouse or your friends will abandon you? Are you afraid you may lose your job? Are you afraid of the future? Some fears are irrational, while others are based on a high probability of truth. Many are somewhere in between. At this stage, don't dwell on your fears; simply identify them. Recognize them for what they are and whom they're from. What are the ways these fears keep you in bondage?

Do keep one important fact in mind: Sometimes the enemy can look bigger than he really is. In chapter 10, for example, we said that hormone fluctuations during our monthly cycles can cause us to feel particularly fearful or suspicious. Certain medications that affect chemical levels in the brain can also make us more susceptible to fearful thinking. Then there's depression, which goes hand in hand with fear. Take a look at your physical health and circumstances and see if any of

So do not fear, for I am with you; do not be dismayed, for I am your God. I will strengthen you and help you; I will uphold you with my righteous right hand. —Isaiah 41:10

these factors may be inducing or magnifying fear—particularly irra-tional fear—in your life. Talk to your doctor about them. Fear is a big enough adversary without hormones, medicines, or the chemicals in our brains inflating it to larger-than-life size.

2. Realize that some things are out of your control.

Once you look your fear in the face, you need to make a realistic determination: What, if anything, can you do about it? If you're worried about theft, for example, you can purchase a home security system or put new locks on your windows and doors. These are things that are within your control. You don't have to go overboard; just take wise pre-cautions.

Some things are not within your control, however, no matter how many precautions you take. That's the case with my daughter's driving. I can make sure Grace gets the best instruction available, and I can set rules and curfews intended for her safety. But an element of hazard will always exist whenever she gets behind the wheel. That's something I have no control over.

The truth is, our world can be a dangerous place, and anything is possible. In most areas of life, we don't have complete control—whether we're talking about job security, a spouse's faithfulness, or an airplane ride. We can be wise and realistic and do what we can do, but sometimes what happens next is out of our hands.

3. Relinquish control to God and rest in him.

After you have taken wise precautions, you need to relinquish con-trol over the circumstances to God and rest in his loving care. You and I have no guarantee that the next moment will be free from tragedy. We only know that God will not leave us, whatever comes our way, and that he is working all things together for good. All things may not seem good at the time, but we can rest in the assurance that God is lovingly working in our lives and in our world in bigger ways than we can imagine.

You may be wondering, *If God is with me, then why doesn't he prevent bad things from happening to me and my loved ones?* Certainly, it's hard to comprehend human suffering. We may never understand why some things happen this side of the Pearly Gates. For now we only know that God is with us. He doesn't guarantee that our lives will be pain free; he simply promises to hold us and care for us through the challenges of life. Because he is a God of redemption, we can trust him to take circumstances that seem hopeless and infuse them with hope.

4. Renounce the fear.

Often little fears tend to creep back into our heads, gripping us and stifling us all over again. We need to be ready for this eventuality with prayer and God's Word. When you recognize fear knocking at the door of your mind, answer it with faith in God, saying, "Although I can't control the outcome of this situation, I know God will be with me. Nothing is too difficult for him." Pray, "Lord, help me to have strength for this moment. I trust you and rest in your loving care. Keep me from fear and worry, because I know they don't come from you." Finally, memorize one or more Bible verses that give you courage and strength, and speak them aloud when you're afraid. (You can start with the Bible verse in the Power Point section, or choose one of the other verses from this chapter.)

Putting On Our Armor

Not only is there a strategy for battling fear; God has provided us with protective armor for the fight. This armor is spiritual, because the battle is against a spiritual enemy. Read Ephesians 6:10–18 along with me:

> Finally, be strong in the Lord and in his mighty power. Put on the full armor of God so that you can take your stand against the devil's schemes. For our struggle is not against flesh and blood, but against the rulers, against the authorities, against the powers of this dark world and against the spiritual forces of evil in the heavenly realms. Therefore put on the full armor of God, so that when the day of evil comes, you may be able to stand your ground, and after you have done everything, to stand. Stand firm then, with the belt of truth buckled around your waist, with the breastplate of righteousness in place, and with your feet fitted with the readiness that comes from the gospel of peace. In addition to all this, take up the shield of faith, with which you can extinguish all the flaming arrows of the evil one. Take the helmet of salvation and the sword of the Spirit, which is the word of God. And pray in the Spirit on all occasions with all kinds of prayers and requests. With this in mind, be alert and always keep on praying for all the saints.

When Paul delivered this message, he was addressing Christians who were facing persecution for their faith—a very real and present danger in those days. No doubt many of the Ephesian believers were struggling with fear. But God spoke these words through Paul to strengthen and encourage the Ephesians, and by extension, to strengthen and encourage us in our own spiritual battles. I like to use the words of this passage as a prayer for myself and for my family members, asking God to equip us with his armor for our daily battles and help us to stand firm against the enemy. Let's take a brief look at each piece of our spiritual battle gear.

The belt of truth. In Bible times the belt was an important part of a soldier's armor, because it was used to hold battle tools. For us, the belt of truth is vital because it holds the one tool we can use to overcome Satan's lies. The Bible says that Satan is "a liar and the father of lies." Sometimes his lies sound true, and they tend to instill fear. But believers have the truth of God's Word—and God's truth always flushes out and defeats the enemy's deceit.

The breastplate of righteousness. The purpose of the breastplate in ancient armor was to guard the heart of the soldier. Satan often attacks us by appealing to our hearts, the seat of our emotions. If we pursue God's righteousness and apply his pure principles of life, however, our hearts will be protected, and Satan cannot to lead us astray.

Feet fitted with the readiness that comes from the gospel of peace. Some soldiers in the Roman army of Jesus' day had spikes in the bottom of their shoes to help them stand their ground. For our own protection, our feet and our very lives should be firmly planted in the gospel message of Jesus Christ—the good news of who he is and what he has done for us. We need to be ready at all times to share that good news and never hesitate to tell others about the peace that comes from having a relationship with God through his Son, Jesus.

The shield of faith. The shield was used to protect the soldier from the attack of the enemy's weapons. Our faith in God is the shield that withstands the flaming arrows of our enemy, Satan. He hurls temptations, fears, lies, and destruction toward us, but our unswerving faith in a loving, all-powerful God is an impenetrable defense.

The helmet of salvation. The helmet was worn to protect the soldier's head—his most vital area besides the heart. Satan tries to use our minds as a destructive force, filling us with fearful doubts and temptations. He particularly wants us to doubt God's salvation and love for us.

We protect our minds with the assurance of salvation that comes from God's Word.

The sword of the Spirit, which is the word of God. This is the only tool used for the offensive battle mentioned in this passage. Jesus used the Word of God as a sword to cut down each one of Satan's temptations in the wilderness (see Matthew 4:1–11). We, too, can respond to Satan's lies and schemes with the weapon of God's Word, which is always true. That's why it's important for us not only to study the Bible, but also to memorize Scripture verses that we can call upon in the midst of battle.

Paul encourages us to use every part of our spiritual armor in order to resist Satan's attacks and stand firm in God. Notice that he tells us to pray at all times and in all situations. In spiritual warfare, we need to stay alert and persist in our prayers for ourselves, our families, and Christians everywhere. In fact, when we face our fears, this is a good battle cry: "Stay alert, and keep praying!" We stay alert by taking wise and realistic precautions when it is within our power to do so. We also stay alert by recognizing that our enemy, Satan, "prowls around like a roaring lion looking for someone to devour" (1 Peter 5:8). Knowing this, we pray for God's protection and power and place our challenges and fears in our heavenly Father's loving hands. Then we stand firm, resisting the temptation to let fear set up camp in our hearts or minds.

Our Deliverer

In the last chapter I mentioned my friend Leslie, whose daughter suffered a critical and life-threatening liver injury in a go-cart accident. Leslie says that while she doesn't understand why God allowed this accident to happen (or why he allowed any of the other tragedies she has faced in the last two years), she did feel God's complete comfort and strength in the midst of it. She says she literally felt a warm blanket

No passion so effectually robs the mind of all its powers of acting and reasoning as fear. —Edmund Burke

216

of God's love covering her throughout the entire ordeal, from the ICU to her daughter's long recovery at home.

Asking God, "Why?" is not necessarily wrong, as long as we realize that we may not get an answer. As Job recognized (you can read his story in the book of the Bible that bears his name), we finite human beings can't begin to understand all of the ways of our great, all-knowing Creator. We can only rest in the fact that our awesome and powerful God is able to bear us up through the storms of life. Psalm 34:17–19 says, "The righteous cry out, and the LORD hears them; he delivers them from all their troubles. The LORD is close to the brokenhearted and saves those who are crushed in spirit. A righteous man may have many troubles, but the LORD delivers him from them all." Does this verse promise we'll have no troubles in life? No, it promises that God will deliver us in the midst of them.

What about my friend Lynn, who lost her daughter to leukemia? Did God deliver her family from their troubles? If you were to ask Lynn if God was there when she faced the biggest fear any parent could face—the loss of a child—she would tell you, "Yes, God delivered us. He held us all in his loving hands, especially when he ushered our daughter into his kingdom." None of us knows what the future holds, but we do know the one who holds the future—and he's the same one who holds us right now. We can trust him, even when we don't understand everything that's going on around us.

In Matthew 6:25–27 Jesus says, "Do not worry about your life, what you will eat or drink; or about your body, what you will wear.... Who of you by worrying can add a single hour to his life?" The number of days of our lives on earth (and those of our children, spouse, and friends) is in God's hands, not ours. Our worries and fears can't add a single hour to even one day! Instead of useless worrying, we need to spend our time listening for the voice of God as he continually tells us,

"Do not fear; do not worry. I am the Good Shepherd who tenderly watches over his flock. I have my eye on you." Whatever fears we may face in life, we can trust him to be with us and to deliver us.

"I'm Taking Off My Skis"

My friend Dana affectionately uses the words, "I'm taking off my skis," with her dad whenever she is facing a tough challenge and needs encouragement and strength. I'll let her tell you in her own words where that phrase originated:

One of the most valuable lessons I have learned in life occurred on a ski slope when I was about twelve years old. It had been a long day and I was tired, wet, and cold. My feet were killing me, and I had fallen more than my fair share of times. As my dad and I glided along an easy path, we came to an opening. I was relieved, thinking that I was just minutes away from a warm fire, dry socks, and a soft sofa. But then I saw that there was one last price to be paid for my comfort: There between me and the bottom of the mountain was one more slope. I don't remember its level of difficulty, but in my mind it was a dreaded black diamond. It had more moguls than Moses would care to part, and I could imagine the imprint of my behind on each one of them.

That was it! I wasn't about to tackle any more hills that day, so I came up with a plan to solve the problem: I would simply take off my skis and walk down. My dad had already started skiing down the hill but stopped and looked back to see if I was coming. I called out, "I'm taking off my skis and walking down."

"No you're not," he replied firmly.

"But dad, I'm tired, and I can't make it," I pleaded.

"C'mon, just follow me," he said confidently.

My dad is the kind of person that when he told you to do something, you didn't stop to think about it; you just did it. With tears streaming down my face, I began the descent. Side to side we went. When I fell, he stopped and waited, and then we slowly continued on. It wasn't easy and I fell many times, but I made it down that hill. The funny thing is that when I looked at it from the bottom, it didn't seem as big or as difficult as it did from the top.

I've had many more hills to conquer since then, and sometimes they seem overwhelming. But I know that my heavenly Father is waiting for me just ahead, saying, "C'mon, follow me." It may not be easy, and I may fall, but he will be there to pick me up and encourage me.

Now whenever I am fearful of something or feel like quitting, I call my dad and say, "I'm taking off my skis." He faithfully reminds me that God is there, and he will get me down the mountain.[4]

What about you, dear sister? What scary slopes are you looking down that seem too difficult to tackle? What fears have paralyzed you, convincing you that you have neither the faith nor the strength to make it to safety and comfort? Remember your heavenly Father is right there with you. If you will trust yourself to his wise guidance and loving care, he will help you make it down that mountain of fear and into the valley of peace, joy, and abundant life.

God is with you, positive woman of faith! Fear not!

POWER POINT

🌸 **Read:** The entire book of Esther. (It's not that long, and it's definitely an interesting story about a woman who faced her fear.) Describe the real and present danger that threatened the Israelite nation. What wise and courageous preventative steps did Esther take? Whom did she depend upon for the ultimate outcome of the situation?

♡ **Pray:** Glorious King of heaven, you are worthy of praise and honor. You are always upholding me with your righteous right hand. Thank you for reminding me continually in your Word to not be afraid, because you are with me. What comfort I have in you! Help me to face the fears in my life that stifle me and keep me from moving forward in faith. I relinquish them to you and ask that you would replace them with your peace. Help me to fear not! I love you, Lord. In Jesus' name I pray, amen.

💡 **Remember:** "God is our refuge and strength, an ever-present help in trouble. Therefore we will not fear" (Psalm 46:1–2).

☺ **Do:** Take a few moments to identify areas in your life that are currently stifled by fear. What reasonable actions or precautions can you take to help reduce your concerns? In prayer, deliver to God those factors that are out of your control. Relinquish them to his hands, trusting him for the outcome.

Every morning, make a conscious effort to "put on" the armor of God. Stay alert, and refuse to allow fearful thoughts to set up camp in your mind or heart.

Power Principle #7

Becoming A Woman of Hope

Optimism is the faith that leads to achievement.
Nothing can be done without hope or confidence.

—Helen Keller

Put your hope in the LORD,
for with the LORD is unfailing love
and with him is full redemption.

—Psalm 130:7

Stop Whining and Start Smiling
Wearing the Bright Glasses of Hope

Behind the cloud the starlight lurks,
Through showers the sunbeams fall;
For God, who loveth all His works,
Has left His hope with all!

—John Greenleaf Whittier

The funeral of former Soviet leader Leonid Brezhnev would not seem to be a likely place to find hope, yet a glimmer of hope was there. The story is told of Brezhnev's widow, who stood by his coffin until just before it was closed. As the soldiers touched the lid, she reached down and made the sign of the cross on her husband's chest—an obvious act of civil disobedience in this stronghold of atheistic power. In this one act, Brezhnev's wife provided a courageous and beautiful picture of hope. Clearly, she hoped for life beyond the grave. She hoped for mercy. She hoped for salvation. And she based this hope on a man who died on a cross two thousand years ago.[1]

The message of the Bible is a message of hope. Hope is not simply a sense of expectation, because you can expect good things or bad things to happen. No, hope is a yearning for something wonderful to happen; it is a looking forward to the best. This is the kind of hope we have as Christians based on our faith in Christ. We have the anticipation of eternal life with Christ in our heavenly home, despite whatever challenges and difficulties we experience in our life on earth. We have the expectation that all things will work together for our good if we love God and are called according to his purpose (see Romans 8:28). We have the hopefulness of knowing that God is at work in our lives through the sad moments as well as the happy ones. First Peter 1:3–7 describes the vibrant hope believers are meant to experience:

> Praise be to the God and Father of our Lord Jesus Christ! In his great mercy he has given us new birth into a living hope through the resurrection of Jesus Christ from the dead, and into an inheritance that can never perish, spoil or fade—kept in heaven for you, who through faith are shielded by God's power until the coming of the salvation that is ready to be revealed in the last time. In this you greatly rejoice, though now for a little while you may have had to suffer grief in all kinds of trials. These have come so that your faith—of greater worth than gold, which perishes even though refined by fire—may be proved genuine and may result in praise, glory and honor when Jesus Christ is revealed.

Yes, we have a living hope—a hope that is in God and his salvation through his son, Jesus. It's a hope that cannot be taken away from us. Even when a loved one dies, we grieve, but not as those who have no hope; for we know we will see that person again one day. How hopeless life must seem to those who have no understanding of our great and loving God, who has an ultimate plan for this world and for our lives! And how joyless! The words *hope* and *joy* are often found together in Scripture for good reason. Romans 5:1–2 spells out why Christians can rejoice in hope: "Since we have been justified through faith, we have peace with God through our Lord Jesus Christ, through whom we have gained access by faith into this grace in which we now stand. And we rejoice in the hope of the glory of God."

Christians ought to be the most optimistic people in the world. After all, we are the ones who have the one true hope! But believers can

Be joyful in hope, patient in affliction, faithful in prayer. —Romans 12:12

fall into the trap of hoping in the here and now, in what can be seen and felt, just like everyone else. Many people put their hope in wealth or fame or perfect circumstances, expecting these things to bring them life and joy and strength. But in his letter to Timothy, Paul warns against hoping in such things: "Command those who are rich in this present world not to be arrogant nor to put their hope in wealth, which is so uncertain, but to put their hope in God, who richly provides us with everything for our enjoyment" (1 Timothy 6:17). Hope is only as good as the one in whom it is placed. We can be confident in our hope when our hope is in the Lord.

Another story of hope set in the former Soviet Union is told of Alexander Solzhenitsyn, a Soviet political prisoner around the middle of the twentieth century. Forced to work twelve-hour days of hard labor while existing on a meager diet, Solzhenitsyn was on the verge of giving up all hope. He was starving and gravely ill, and the doctors were predicting his death. One afternoon, as he was shoveling sand in the hot sun, he simply stopped working. He knew the guards would beat him severely, but he just couldn't go on. It was then that he saw a fellow Christian prisoner cautiously moving toward him. The man quickly drew a cross in the sand with his cane and then erased it. In that brave gesture of love and encouragement, all the hope of the Gospel flooded Solzhenitsyn's soul. That hope helped him endure that difficult day as well as the months and years of prison life that followed.[2]

The hope of the cross is powerful. It is the hope that Christ paid the price for our salvation. It is the hope that Christ rose from the dead and that the same power that raised him from the dead is at work in our lives. We can rejoice in this hope, and we can rest in it. As the writer of Hebrews said, "We have this hope as an anchor for the soul, firm and secure" (Hebrews 6:19).

Give Up Grumbling

You would think the Israelites would have been an optimistic group of people. The God of the universe had miraculously delivered them from Egyptian slavery. They were headed toward the Promised Land with not only their freedom, but also the riches of Egypt—an extra parting gift from God. You would think they would have easily put their hope in the Lord and his provision, but they didn't. Instead, they got caught up in their own temporary discomforts and difficulties. Granted, the tents in the wilderness were no Ritz Carlton. But incredible satisfaction and joy were just ahead, waiting for them just over the Jordan. Sadly, the Israelites chose to whine and complain about their circumstances rather than trust God and put their hope in his promises.

How did God feel about their pessimistic complaining? Numbers 11:1 says, "Now the people complained about their hardships in the hearing of the LORD, and when he heard them his anger was aroused." God was not happy about their grumbling because it exposed their lack of faith. It was destructive, killing their hope and interfering with God's plan to bless them.

What about us? Are we much different from the whining Israelites? What do we tend to grumble and whine about in our temporary journey here on earth? No doubt God feels the same way about our grumbling as he did the Israelites'. Paul tells us in Philippians 2:14 to "do all things without grumbling" (NASB). Yet most of us tend to ignore this guideline and chatter on and on about our problems.

Grumbling is an unproductive use of our time, words, and energy. When we whine and complain, we encourage doubt instead of faith. We take our eyes off of the hope we have in God and place them on immediate issues and temporary things. Of course there may be times when we see something that is wrong and need to take action to make a positive change, but we can do this without grumbling.

Romans 12:12 gives us a remedy for grumbling: "Be joyful in hope, patient in affliction, faithful in prayer." Next time you feel a whine or complaint coming on, take a dose of Romans 12:12 instead! It may seem silly, but I recommend putting an empty medicine bottle on the kitchen counter with a label that reads:

> *Rx: Grumble Squelchers*
>
> *Reduces symptoms of whining, complaining, and fretting.*
> *Take at first sign of bellyaching.*

Write out Romans 12:12 on a strip of paper and put it inside the bottle. Then when you feel like grumbling, pop the top and follow the directions:

1. Be joyful in hope. This means that we take pleasure and find joy in our expectation that God is mightily at work in our lives. We know that our future is bright as we look forward to a heavenly home.

2. Be patient in affliction. Because we have hope in God, we can be patient when life gets difficult. We know that our present circumstances are only temporary; they *will* pass. According to James 1:2–4, we can even be joyful when we face trials and struggles, because they test our faith and develop perseverance—a quality that's necessary if we're going to become mature, complete, and positive women of faith.

3. Be faithful in prayer. We can't avoid all pain and difficulty in life, but we can allow these things to mature us as we persevere in joyful hope and faithful prayer. As we deliver our dilemmas and defeats to God in daily prayer, he is faithful to give us wisdom, direction, comfort, and strength. Imagine what would happen if you and I decided to spend more time praying and less time grumbling and complaining. We would become much more positive, joyful, and hopeful people, and everyone around us would clamor to know the one in whom we place our hope.

She Wore Bright Glasses

I'm sure you know the story of Helen Keller. Born in 1880, she contracted a severe illness in infancy that left her in a dark world void of sound and sight. Unable to communicate, she became an angry and frustrated child—until hope came into her life in the form of a teacher named Anne Sullivan. Helen learned to read, write, and speak through Anne's patient and loving instruction. Eventually she graduated cum laude from Radcliffe College, published her life story, and became a well-known and much-honored public figure.

Helen Keller's life represents one of the most extraordinary stories of hope, courage, and perseverance in American history. She may have worn dark glasses in public; but in her spirit and attitude, she clearly wore bright glasses that focused her sights on life's potential rather than life's difficulties. Through these glasses she saw opportunity instead of defeat, hope instead of despair. How is it possible to be hopeful in the face of such immense challenges? Here's the key in Helen's own words: "Keep your face to the sunshine and you cannot see the shadows."[3]

Like Helen, we have a choice as to which "attitude glasses" we will put on each day. Despite our circumstances, we can choose to don the bright glasses of hope, which see God's hand at work in our lives; or we can choose the dark glasses of despair, which only see our immediate troubles. If we wear these dark glasses long enough, we will become hopeless, angry, and bitter people—chronic whiners and grumblers. It's a daily choice. Will we focus on God and his provision, or will we focus on our handicap—whether it's a serious illness, a difficult spouse, an unpleasant work environment, a dysfunctional family, a broken down car? Are we willing to look beyond the handicap and see the possibilities?

God didn't take away Helen's handicaps; he accomplished great things through them. He didn't take away Paul's unnamed handicap, even though Paul asked God three times to remove it. Instead, Paul learned that God's grace was sufficient for him to survive and even thrive in spite of his challenge (see 2 Corinthians 12:7–10). Our difficulties may not go away, either, but that doesn't mean God is not with us. He is able to work in us and through us, no matter what struggles we face.

And therein lies our hope. Hope goes beyond what we see and feel in the here and now. Romans 8:24–25 says, "Hope that is seen is no hope at all. Who hopes for what he already has? But if we hope for what we do not yet have, we wait for it patiently." Have hope in God! His work in us is not finished. As one person put it, "Hope is putting faith to work when doubting would be easier.[4]"

It's All in Your Perspective

Here's a little poem about a frog with a hope-filled perspective:

Two frogs fell into a deep cream bowl,
One was quite an optimistic soul;
But the other took the gloomy view,
"We shall drown," he cried, without ado.
So with a last despairing cry,
He flung up his legs and he said, "Goodbye."
Quoth the other frog with a merry grin,
"I can't get out, but I won't give in.
I'll just swim till my strength is spent,
Then will I die the more content."
Bravely he swam till it would seem
His struggles began to churn the cream.
On the top of the butter at last he stopped,

And out of the bowl he gaily hopped.

What of the moral? 'Tis easily found:

If you can't hop out, keep swimming round.[5]

When it comes to hope, perspective is everything! One frog lost hope and died in a bowl of cream; the other hoped for the best, did what he could, and ended up climbing out of his troubles. Hope kept him going—and it keeps us going too. With a bright outlook and an eternal perspective, we can see past the small stuff. We can keep ourselves from getting weighed down in the cream of life.

I think about a woman I know who has a marvelous singing voice. Unfortunately, she continually wrings her hands in defeat, telling herself, "I'll never be a singer. No one will help me get the big break I need. I don't have connections in the industry. I think I'll quit." She's lost in the cream. Hope says, "There are opportunities all around you to use your talent. Yes, the audiences are small and the stages are not lighted, but you still can be a blessing to many people." Hope says, "God has a plan for your life. If you will step through the open doors that are in front of you and keep your eyes on the Lord, he will lead you to greater heights than you could even imagine."

When we lose hope, we sink. But even then God is there to lift us up; we just have to reach out for his hand. Matthew 14:22–33 tells the story of Jesus walking across the water to meet his disciples, who were in a boat on a lake in the middle of a storm. When Peter saw Jesus, he boldly called out, "Lord, if it's you, tell me to come to you on the water." Jesus replied, "Come." So Peter stepped out of the boat and started walking—that is, until he noticed the raging wind and crashing waves around him. Becoming afraid, he immediately started to sink. But before he went all the way under, he managed to cry out, "Lord, save me!" Jesus responded by reaching out his hand and pulling Peter to safety. "You of little faith, why did you doubt?" he said to his very wet disciple.

Peter started out with his hope in the Lord. He didn't hesitate to get out of the boat when Jesus said, "Come." But then Peter got his focus off of Jesus and onto the wind and the waves—and he sank. Been there? It's so easy to lose perspective. Life's difficulties and challenges perplex us and distract us on every side, pulling our focus away from the Lord and the hope we have in him. Like Peter, when we take our eyes off of Jesus and put them on our circumstances, we begin sinking into despair. But also like Peter, when we reach out in hope to the one who loves us and has the power to save us, we experience miracles!

Keep Smiling

I love Emily Dickinson's words about hope: "Hope is the thing with feathers that perches in the soul and sings the tune without words and never stops at all."[6] When we have hope within us, it overflows like a fountain to those around us. It lifts people's spirits like a never-ending song, inspiring them to hope too.

How do we share hope? We'll talk about this more in the next chapter, but what I want to emphasize here is that it's not difficult. Sometimes it takes little more than a smile. Proverbs 15:13 tells us, "A happy heart makes the face cheerful." As women of hope, we ought to have joyful, hopeful hearts. We have reason to smile! We can smile at today, because we know that a greater day is coming. We can smile at the future, because we know the one who holds the future. A smile is like a gift of hope we offer to others. It speaks a thousand words, saying, "It will be okay. There is a better day ahead. God is with us."

Abraham Lincoln said, "I have found that most people are about as happy as they make up their minds to be."[7] The question is, how happy do you want to be? Will you choose today to put on the glasses of hope

As God is the author of our salvation, so Christ is the embodiment of our hope. —Geoffrey B. Wilson

in God, or will you wear the glasses of gloom in circumstances? Will you smile more and grumble less, or will it be the other way around?

In the August 5, 2001, issue of *Parade* magazine, a small article appeared about a Texas-based group called the Secret Society of Happy People. The article noted that happy people generally aren't invited to tell their stories on TV talk shows, even though studies have proven that a positive outlook can lead to a longer life. The Society of Happy People declared August to be "Admit You Are Happy Month." Their hope was that the month of good cheer would rub off on people, and everyone would spend less time thinking and talking about what makes them miserable.

As women of hope, we should declare every day "Admit You Are Hopeful Day." The psalmist said, "Why are you downcast, O my soul? Why so disturbed within me? Put your hope in God, for I will yet praise him, my Savior and my God" (Psalm 43:5). You and I have reason to put away doom and gloom and be glad: God, through Christ, has given us a living and lasting hope. As Thomas Manton said, "What an excellent ground of hope and confidence we have when we reflect upon these three things in prayer: the Father's love, the Son's merit, and the Spirit's power!"[8] Let's make a daily choice to share that hope with the world.

POWER POINT

Read: The story of the Shunammite woman's hope in 2 Kings 4:8–37. What positive qualities do you see in this woman? What did she do when it seemed as though all hope was gone for her son? Notice that she told no one about her son's death; instead, she went straight to the prophet of God. What can be learned from her example?

Pray: God of hope, I praise you for your Word and your power, which give me hope for the journey of life. Thank you for my greatest hope: that I will live with you one day in glory. Renew my hope, and help me to keep an eternal perspective. Today and every day, help me to choose an attitude of hope rather than an attitude of gloom or despair. Teach me to be joyful in hope, patient in affliction, and faithful in prayer. In Christ's name, amen.

💡 **Remember:** "Be joyful in hope, patient in affliction, faithful in prayer" (Romans 12:12).

☺ **Do:** Write out a statement of hope. Make it a personal reminder of hope, based on God's truth. It may sound something like this:

> My hope is based on the fact that God loves me and sent his Son, Jesus, to die on the cross as a payment for my sins. He rose again, giving me hope for eternal life. I have hope for each day because I know that God is working all things in my life together for good, as Romans 8:28 promises to those who love God and are called according to his purpose.

Place your statement of hope in your Bible and refer to it whenever you need to be reminded to get your eyes off of your immediate circumstances and back onto Jesus.

16

Delicious Morsels
Serving Up a Hearty Portion of
Hope and Encouragement

*Believe that your tender, loving thoughts and wishes for good have
power to help the struggling souls of earth to rise higher.*

—Ella Wheeler-Wilcox

Abigail Van Buren occasionally shares stories of "random acts of kindness" sent in by readers of her popular column, "Dear Abby." Recently she printed a letter from a woman from Long Island who was reflecting on a visit she made some time ago to Albuquerque, New Mexico. The purpose of the woman's trip was to be alone and finally accept the fact that her husband had died. This was her first vacation without him. As she sat by herself in a lovely restaurant, she noticed a corner table being prepared near hers, complete with a fresh flower arrangement and champagne bucket. Soon a couple was escorted to the table. She recognized the man immediately as a famous personality. She tried not to glance at the couple too often as she sat nearby, alone and forlorn.

To her surprise, a server approached her and said, "The couple at the corner table would like to send a glass of champagne to you." When he asked if that would be all right, she graciously accepted. Then, catching the couple's attention, she lifted her glass appreciatively and toasted them on their special occasion.

The famous gentleman leaned toward her and said, "It's not a special occasion, just a celebration of life—to the good times ahead."

In her letter to "Dear Abby," the woman said that whenever she feels blue, she reflects on that special couple and their "celebration of life." Abby commented, "People who are happy are usually inclined to spread the joy."[1]

That couple in New Mexico offered a glimmer of hope to a needy soul that night. Sending the glass of champagne was a small act of kindness on their part, but it was a lasting gift to this woman who shared her story with Abby nearly ten years later. We, too, have baskets full of hope that we can share with the world around us. Like the little boy who offered up to Jesus his five loaves and two fish, God can take our simple gifts of hope and multiply them many times over in the lives of others. Never underestimate the power of your words and actions to provide hope to your family, your friends, and everyone around you!

Handing Out Hope

The most satisfying moments in life are those in which we encourage other people to go on to greater heights. When we hand out hope to those we hold dear, we often get to participate in their renewed dreams and become a part of their significant life experiences. When we give hope to those we don't know so well, we may never know the long-term effect; but like the couple in New Mexico, we get to experience the immediate joy of watching the light of hope go on in someone else's eyes.

How do we effectively encourage someone along life's pathway? How do we hand out hope? The answer begins with simple steps— small acts of encouragement and kindness, based on our recognition of the other person's great value and worth in God's eyes. Because every one of us has been uniquely created by God, each person has worth just waiting to be discovered. It may be simple; it may not be newsworthy;

but each person has something to offer; each person has a contribution to make to this world.

We can encourage that God-given potential to bloom and grow by looking deep inside a person and drawing out the good things we see planted there. When we do this, we water that life with hope. We especially need to keep an eye out for those lasting qualities that rarely fade or diminish, like love, joy, peace, patience, kindness, goodness, faithfulness, gentleness, and self-control. These are qualities that God develops through the work of his Holy Spirit, and they are ones we particularly want to encourage in others.

Teachers, managers, bosses, coaches, and especially mothers have opportunities built in to their daily tasks to encourage potential and inspire hope. Baseball legend Reggie Jackson describes an uplifting manager this way: "A great manager has a knack for making ballplayers think they are better than they think they are. He forces you to have a good opinion of yourself. He lets you know he believes in you. He makes you get more out of yourself. And once you learn how good you really are, you never settle for playing anything less than your very best."[2]

Wouldn't it be wonderful if we, as positive women, regularly gave this kind of encouragement and hope to the people around us? If we always looked for and drew out the good qualities, abilities, and talents in others? What a blessing it would be to hear people say, "That Karol Ladd, she has a knack for making people think they are better than they are. She forces them to have a good opinion about themselves. Yes, she lets people know she believes in them!" Our world would be a better place if we took the time and made the effort to help others recognize their worth. As Goethe said, "Treat people as if they were what they should be, and you help them become what they are capable of becoming."[3]

Apples of Gold

"A word aptly spoken is like apples of gold in settings of silver," says Solomon in Proverbs 25:11. According to the Bible, words are both valuable and powerful. They can be lovely and life-giving, or they can be sour and destructive. They can be the tools by which we build a future, encourage a dream, or unleash great potential; or they can be the weapons by which we destroy a reputation, diminish a self-image, or quench an inner fire. If you think back, you can probably remember times when words spoken by others either empowered you or discouraged you. As positive women, we need to be life-givers with our words!

I remember the first time my husband heard me speak to a large group of men and women. I had spoken on this particular topic many times before, but I was extremely nervous at the thought of Curt being there. What if I told a joke that flopped? What if I went completely blank? What if the material was dry? When the talk was over, I would have to live my life—for better or for worse—with a member of the audience! (Did I mention that Curt is very blunt and doesn't mind speaking the truth in love, even if it hurts?) Fortunately the talk went well, and people laughed in all the right places. Curt darted up to me afterward and said, "You were fantastic! I knew you were good, but I didn't know you were this good!" He believed in me! His words of strength gave me hope and encouragement to carry on. They still ring in my mind to this day.

When was the last time you delivered a healthy dose of encouragement to another person? Words of hope can be delivered in many forms. Not long ago I noticed that I was continually on my teenage daughter's case for every little issue. (She noticed it too.) Knowing how powerful words are, and realizing that I was nitpicking her over some pretty unimportant things, I determined to change. First, I decided to only concern myself with what was really important and relax about the small stuff. Second, I decided to make sure I gave her words of hope every day.

I already had the habit of telling her "I love you" several times a day. Now I began telling her at other times, "Grace, I believe in you." "Grace, God has a wonderful plan for your life." "Grace, God is going to bless you and use your gifts and talents." I began giving my other daughter similar words of hope: "Joy, you have a kind and tender servant's heart that is such a blessing to me and to others." "Joy, it's beautiful to see how God's love shines through you." "Joy, God is working in mighty ways in your life." Over time I began to see courage, discipline, and a renewed zest for life rising in both my girls.

Years ago a song hit the charts with the lyric, "Accentuate the positive, eliminate the negative." I've found that as I focus on the positive qualities of the people around me and feed them words of encouragement, their best qualities tend to develop and grow. In the process their negative qualities tend to take care of themselves and diminish in prominence. Dishing out delicious morsels of hope to my family strengthens them greatly—and brings me great pleasure. Encouraging words help my kids and my husband rise to their potential, and they give me a lift too!

Of course, words of hope and encouragement don't always have to be verbal. Sometimes I find it easier to write a note of encouragement to a friend than to pick up the phone and call. That's okay. The written word is powerful! I have a file at my house that I've labeled, "Encouraging Words." In it I place the kind, supportive, and meaningful notes and letters I receive from people. Some are from friends; others are from people who have heard me speak or who've read my books. Their words of encouragement are a source of great strength and hope to me. Even in the process of writing this book, I received several letters from readers of my previous book, *The Power of a Positive Mom*. Their

May the God of hope fill you with all joy and peace as you trust in him, so that you may overflow with hope by the power of the Holy Spirit. —Romans 15:13

notes were an inspiration, particularly at those times (every writer has them!) when I felt dry or discouraged. These letters spurred me on to complete the task that was before me. You hold the end result in your hands!

Hope Floats

A few years ago actress Sandra Bullock starred in a movie by Twentieth Century Fox titled *Hope Floats.* The film begins with Sandra's character being invited to appear on a sleazy talk show where, in front of a national television audience, she finds out that her husband is having an affair with her best friend. Distraught and broken, she decides to take her young daughter and move back to her mother's house in her old hometown. There, in the small, quaint town of Smithville, she starts to work through her grief and begins to see glimmers of hope in her life. Her family and friends stand with her, encourage her, and let her know they believe in her through this process. They shower her with hope. It takes time, it's not easy, it doesn't happen the way she planned; but eventually hope wins out, and Sandra's character finds the peace and joy she is searching for.

Most of the people we know and love are not likely to have their lives turned upside down by a revelation on national television, but they will have their share of difficulties and challenges. We need to tell them: There is hope! Hope for a better day. Hope for eternal life. Hope that God can take even the bad experiences and somehow use them for good. As we sit alongside a hurting or struggling person, sometimes the only thing we can give them to hold on to is the fact that God is with them, and he loves them. He will give them strength moment by moment. And as they persevere, trusting in him, they will become better, stronger, and more positive people.

The following poem by an anonymous author says it well:

The Hard Way

For every hill I've had to climb,
For every stone that bruised my feet,
For all the blood and sweat and grime,
For blinding storms and burning heat,
My heart sings but a grateful song—
These were the things that made me strong![4]

Many times I have used science experiments to demonstrate lessons in my talks to women. One *egg*cellent *egg*speriment comes from—you guessed it—the egg. Did you know that you can make an egg float? Try this: Place an egg in a bowl of water. It slowly sinks to the bottom, right? Now take the egg out of the bowl for a moment, add salt to the water, and gently stir. *Voila,* you have salt water. And because salt water has a greater density than plain water, the egg will now float when you place it back in the bowl.

Jesus told his followers they were "the salt of the earth" (Matthew 5:13). Salt has many wonderful qualities. In our *egg*speriment we saw that it can buoy up a sinking egg—much like our message of hope can lift a sinking soul. Salt also seasons and preserves. Paul tells us in Colossians 4:6, "Let your conversation be always full of grace, seasoned with salt, so that you may know how to answer everyone." Our words to others can be powerful, life-giving, and uplifting tools in God's hands. When they are full of his grace and truth, hope floats!

Beautiful Feet

My dear friend Beth is a positive woman and a true encouragement to me. We laugh together about many things. One time, as we were bantering back and forth about the qualities we have that we could brag about, Beth said that one of her finer qualities was that she had great-looking feet!

241

We agreed this wasn't the kind of information she'd want to put on her application for Woman of the Year; but to this day, we laugh about her outstanding physical quality. She does have lovely toes!

Did you know that the Bible talks about people with beautiful feet? Yes, you and I can have beautiful feet too. (Watch out, Beth!) Isaiah 52:7 says, "How beautiful on the mountains are the feet of those who bring good news, who proclaim peace, who bring good tidings, who proclaim salvation, who say to Zion, 'Your God reigns!'" Paul quotes this passage in his letter to the Romans, speaking about the power of our words in sharing the gospel message:

> That if you confess with your mouth, "Jesus is Lord," and believe in your heart that God raised him from the dead, you will be saved. For it is with your heart that you believe and are justified, and it is with your mouth that you confess and are saved. As the Scripture says, "Anyone who trusts in him will never be put to shame." For there is no difference between Jew and Gentile—the same Lord is Lord of all and richly blesses all who call on him, for, "everyone who calls on the name of the Lord will be saved."
>
> How, then, can they call on the one they have not believed in? And how can they believe in the one of whom they have not heard? And how can they hear without someone preaching to them? And how can they preach unless they are sent? As it is written, "How beautiful are the feet of those who bring good news!" (Romans 10:9–15)

The greatest hope we can deliver to another person is the hope we have in God through Christ Jesus. When we share the Gospel, our words become a message of peace to those who are restless, a message of love to those who are angry, and a message of hope to those who are hopeless. We offer them healing and wholeness as we share the good news that they, too, can be reconciled to God through faith in his Son, Jesus. Peter tell us, "Always be prepared to give an answer to everyone who asks you to give the reason for the hope that you have" (1 Peter 3:15). If we ask God to open our eyes to see the myriad of opportunities we have to share the reason for our hope, and if we then open our mouths to speak that truth in love, we will have beautiful feet (metaphorically speaking, of course). Why should Beth be the only one?

A Charlie Brown Perspective

Over the years my friend Peni has sent me a variety of fun e-mails. One recent one was a two-part quiz that I found particularly interesting. She prefaced the e-mail by saying that I didn't need to actually answer the questions; I just needed to read the quiz through to get the point. It was purportedly developed by Charles Schulz, the creator of the comic strip "Peanuts." Here it is:

1. Name the five wealthiest people in the world.

2. Name the last five Heisman Trophy winners.

3. Name the last five winners of the Miss America contest.

4. Name ten people who have won the Nobel or Pulitzer Prize.

5. Name the last half-dozen Academy Award winners for best actor and actress.

6. Name the last decade's worth of World Series winners.

How did you do? Probably about as badly as I did! Now see how you do on this second part:

1. List a few teachers who aided your journey through school.

2. Name three friends who have helped you through a difficult time.

3. Name five people who have taught you something worthwhile.

4. Think of a few people who have made you feel appreciated and special.

5. Think of five people you enjoy spending time with.

6. Name half a dozen heroes whose stories have inspired you.

That was quite a bit easier, wasn't it? That's because the people who make the biggest difference in our lives are not necessarily the ones who have achieved fame or fortune or worldly success; they're the ones who care—the ones who give us hope and encouragement to reach our highest potential.

You and I don't have to be celebrities or national heroes to have a positive impact on others. We only need to offer encouragement through our caring smiles, our loving touches, our words of hope—and even our supportive cheers. Recently my daughters and I volunteered at a local swimming competition for the Special Olympics. I think the participants in these unique competitions are possibly the most delightful people I have ever met. They are eager, joyful, innocent, and loving individuals who have an amazing knack for rising above their physical and mental challenges. In these races, no one loses!

When we arrived at the Special Olympics that morning, the director of the volunteers instructed us to go to the edge of the pool, help the participants out of the water after each race, and then chaperone them to the awards ceremony. But when we got to the pool, we saw that many volunteers were already helping in that capacity. Someone directed us further, "Stand at the top of a lane and cheer the swimmer on." So Joy, Grace, and I took our positions at different lanes and began to cheer.

Have you noticed that it's hard to cheer and cry tears of joy at the same time? Over and over my eyes welled up as I was moved by the

The word which God has written on the brow of every man is Hope. —Victor Hugo

courage of the contestants. I could only imagine that for many of them, it had taken every ounce of courage they could muster to get into the water initially, much less learn to swim and eventually compete. All had disabilities to one degree or another; some had to be lowered into the water from their wheelchairs. Every stroke took intense energy and strength, yet they bravely completed their laps without complaint. The smiles of joy that beamed from their faces brought tears of joy to mine.

For three and a half hours, the girls and I cheered our hearts out! We hugged these wonderful Olympians and didn't mind at all getting soaked with each embrace. When we left that day, we knew we were not the same people. We saw life from a new perspective now. What had seemed like major challenges in our lives looked rather minor in this new light. The dilemma of which high school homecoming dress to buy paled in comparison to the struggle of an Olympian deciding which shoe went on the right foot.

Our day at the Special Olympics taught us that we could press on courageously in spite of difficulties. It taught us we could finish our course without complaining. After all, we really had very little to complain about! It also taught us that a cheerleader's role is just as important as a scorekeeper's—maybe even more so. My daughters and I brought hope to the pool that day in the form of hugs and cheers. We left with a new and hopeful outlook on life, delivered by the examples of these special competitors.

Remember, we don't need to be famous. We don't need to be rich. We don't need to wait for our lives to be trouble free before we begin to encourage other people in theirs. Right now, right where we are, we can begin to dole out delicious morsels of encouragement and hope to our families, our friends, and everyone around us. When we do—when we get our eyes off of ourselves and pour our lives out to others in words and actions and cheers that inspire hope—we can't help but become more hopeful too. And that's when we become truly positive women.

POWER POINT

⚙ **Read:** Mark 5:25–34, the story of a woman's desperate hope. How long had this woman been ill? What measures had she tried to get better, to no avail? Did she give up hope? What did her hope lead her to do? The Greek word for *healed* in verse 34 actually means "saved." Knowing this, how is this story meaningful to you?

♡ **Pray:** I praise you wonderful Lord, for you are truly good. Thank you for bringing your *Son*shine into my life. Thank you for the radiant glow on my face that only comes from you. I want to share those rays of hope with the world around me! Help me to bring hope and encouragement to others through my words and actions, and help me to lead them to you, the source of all hope. In Jesus' wonderful name, amen.

💡 **Remember:** "Put your hope in the LORD, for with the LORD is unfailing love and with him is full redemption" (Psalm 130:7).

☺ **Do:** Make a conscious decision to feed delicious morsels of hope and encouragement to your family and close friends every day. Make a list of specific ways you can do this for each person. Then prayerfully ask God to show you someone outside your close circle of friends to whom you can be an encouragement with words or actions of hope. Remember to pray for that person daily.

Conclusion

Press On!
Making a Powerful Difference

*We have learned that power is a positive force
if it is used for positive purposes.*

—Elizabeth Dole

Beth Anne DeCiantis was determined to qualify for the marathon in the 1992 U.S. Olympic Trials. In order to qualify, a female runner had to complete the 26.2-mile course in less than two hours and forty-five minutes. Beth started the race strong, but she began having trouble around the twenty-third mile. She reached the final straightaway with just two minutes left to qualify. With only two hundred yards to the finish line, the unthinkable happened: She stumbled and fell. She stayed down for twenty seconds in a bit of a daze with the crowd yelling, "Get up!" The clock was still ticking, and she had just a minute left.

Beth staggered to her feet and slowly began walking. But just five yards short of the finish line and with ten seconds to go, she fell again. With dogged determination she began to crawl, while the crowd cheered her on. She finally crossed the finish line on her hands and knees. Her time? Two hours, forty-four minutes, and fifty-seven seconds.[1]

When the race got tough, Beth Anne DeCiantis persisted. How easy it would have been for her to give up! She had every opportunity to quit, but she didn't. She pressed on in spite of the pain and struggle and reached her goal.

There are times in all of our lives when we want to throw in the towel and say, "Forget it! This is too hard! I want to quit!" We make mistakes, people do things to hurt us, tragedies happen, sadness prevails. We wonder if we can or should go on. Dear sister, press on! As Beth Anne DeCiantis did, as Helen Keller did, as Harriet Tubman did, as Sarah and Esther and Ruth and Mary did, so can we. We only have to live our lives one step at a time. Perseverance is the key to reaching the finish line.

I am reminded of the story of the great missionary William Carey. When Carey began thinking of traveling to India as a pioneer missionary, his father felt it necessary to point out that he had no academic qualifications to prepare him for the task. Carey responded, "I can plod."[2] In many cases the ones who accomplish lasting results for the kingdom and for the good of mankind are not those who can get things done quickly and easily, but rather the plodders who persist through thick and thin. Plod on!

An Unquenchable Spirit

History is replete with the stories of plodders. Although we may not be aware of all the challenges that were involved, many success stories are really stories of people who had persistence and an unquenchable spirit—people who were absolutely determined to reach their goal. You are probably familiar with the following people, but did you know:

- Dr. Seuss's first children's book was rejected by twenty-three publishers.

- The Coca-Cola Company sold only four hundred Cokes in its first year of business.

- In his first three years in the automobile business, Henry Ford went bankrupt twice.

- Robert Frost's poetry was rejected by the poetry editor of the *Atlantic Monthly* in 1902 with a letter saying, "Our magazine has no room for your vigorous verse."

- Michael Jordan was cut from his high school basketball team.

- In 1905 the University of Bern rejected Albert Einstein's Ph.D. dissertation, saying that it was irrelevant and fanciful.

- Joan Benoit underwent knee surgery seventeen days before the U.S. Olympic Trials for the marathon. She not only made the team; she came home with the gold medal.

- Vince Lombardi was forty-seven when he finally became a head coach in the NFL.[3]

What do all of these people have in common? They pressed on! Though they faced discouragement, they did not lose heart. As Christians, we of all people should not give in to discouragement. Paul explains, "Therefore we do not lose heart. Though outwardly we are wasting away, yet inwardly we are being renewed day by day. For our light and momentary troubles are achieving for us an eternal glory that far outweighs them all. So we fix our eyes not on what is seen, but on what is unseen. For what is seen is temporary, but what is unseen is eternal" (2 Corinthians 4:16–18). In other words, we need to keep our eyes on the big, eternal picture and stop sweating the small stuff!

Persisting with Enthusiasm

In 1964 J. V. Cerney wrote a book entitled *How to Develop a Million-Dollar Personality.* In it he described the physiological benefits

Never, never, never give up. —Winston Churchill

of having enthusiasm in life. Here is his "top ten" list, so to speak, of reasons to be enthusiastic:

1. Aids digestion.

2. Improves metabolism.

3. Relieves tension.

4. Improves muscle function.

5. Stimulates circulation.

6. Steps up endocrine action (hormones).

7. Stabilizes the blood pressure.

8. Stimulates a dynamo of energy.

9. Provides a feeling of euphoria (well-being).

10. Establishes reserve power for periods when you are feeling low.[4]

Wow! Did you have any idea enthusiasm was so beneficial to our bodies? But its benefits don't stop there. Enthusiasm plays a big part in what you and I are able to achieve in this world. A survey was given to a group of self-made millionaires, asking them to list and rate the qualities that had contributed to their success. The final tally looked like this:

Ability ....5 percent
Knowledge ....5 percent
Discipline ....10 percent
Attitude ....40 percent
Enthusiasm ....40 percent[5]

Sometimes we can increase our abilities or our knowledge with outside input, but discipline, attitude, and enthusiasm can only come from within. Of course, we all have days when we just don't feel bubbly, springy, or lively. That's okay. In the introduction to this book, I mentioned that the word *enthusiasm* comes from the Greek words *en theos,* meaning "God within." Enthusiasm is not so much an outward quality as it is an inward desire, based on the assurance we have that God is with us and his Holy Spirit is in us. For positive women of faith, enthusiasm is more than its modern definition of an intense or eager interest. Rather, it is a deep longing and persistent desire to use the gifts and talents God has placed in us, knowing that he will give us the strength and power to express them in a positive way that will bless others and glorify him.

Ralph Waldo Emerson said, "Enthusiasm is one of the most powerful engines of success. When you do a thing, do it with your might. Put your whole soul into it. Stamp it with your own personality. Be active, be energetic, be enthusiastic and faithful, and you will accomplish your object."[6] Paul puts it another way, "Work hard and cheerfully at whatever you do, as though you were working for the Lord rather than for people" (Colossians 3:23 NLT).

Each day we can choose whether or not to be enthusiastic in our lives. As the author of several party books, I speak to women quite often on the topic of parties and entertainment. But as I noted in my last book, *The Power of a Positive Mom,* one huge party goes on every day all around the world, and we have a standing invitation: the Ladies Pity Party. Don't accept! Instead of focusing on our problems and circumstances and feeling sorry for ourselves, let's choose to be grateful for God's goodness and hopeful and enthusiastic about the future, knowing that God is with us. He is at work in us at this very moment, and he has great plans in store.

Choose to Move Forward

We all have regrets. We've all made mistakes. We all have all sinned. It's easy to beat ourselves up mentally, telling ourselves that we are foolish, or failures, or not capable or deserving of moving on in life. Yes, God hates sin because he knows how it can ravage our lives. But he doesn't hate us. God is a forgiving God. He is a God of new beginnings. His love and forgiveness can give us the courage to turn from our sin and begin moving again in a positive direction.

The Bible is all about moving forward and not looking back. Paul, who had persecuted Christians in his younger days and had much to regret, said he was forgetting those things that were behind him and moving forward to what was ahead (Philippians 3:12–14). Wallowing in regret is never healthy. We may have remorse or grief over sin for a time, and rightly so; but ultimately we must leave it behind and move on in forgiveness and newness of life.

We can find motivation to move on in the story of the woman who was caught in adultery and brought before Jesus for judgment. Her accusers were the so-called righteous Pharisees, who wanted to trick Jesus in the process of punishing the woman for her sin. The Law of Moses said that a woman caught in adultery must be stoned. Would Jesus go along with that law or get himself into trouble by breaking it? Jesus responded to their challenge by bending down to the ground and writing in the sand with his finger—perhaps writing out the personal sins of the accusers, as some scholars suggest. The story continues:

> When they kept on questioning him, he straightened up and said to them, "If any one of you is without sin, let him be the first to throw a stone at her." Again he stooped down and wrote on the ground.
>
> At this, those who heard began to go away one at a time, the older ones first, until only Jesus was left, with the woman still standing there. Jesus straightened up and asked her, "Woman, where are they? Has no one condemned you?"

Therefore, my beloved brethren, be steadfast, immovable, always abounding in the work of the Lord, knowing that your toil is not in vain in the Lord. —1 Corinthians 15:58 NASB

"No one, sir," she said.

"Then neither do I condemn you," Jesus declared. "Go now and leave your life of sin." (John 8:7–11)

Let's be quite clear: Jesus was not condoning adultery. He spoke strongly against it on other occasions (see Matthew 5:27–30 and 19:18). Rather, his message to this woman was to stop sinning and move on. Is there sin that needs to be dealt with in your life? Stop reading right now and take those sins before the Father, confessing them and asking for his forgiveness. Ask him to give you the strength to turn from them and to stay turned from them. You can do this confidently, knowing that God is faithful and just to forgive you of your sins and cleanse you from all unrighteousness (see 1 John 1:9). Now go and sin no more!

Satan, our enemy, is an accuser. He would love to disarm our enthusiasm and thwart our potential in life by bombarding us with guilt and regret. When we find ourselves being attacked with debilitating thoughts, we need to put on our armor (as we learned in chapter 14). We need to hold up our shield of faith, knowing that Jesus took care of our sins on the cross, and we are forgiven completely.

Of course, we shouldn't be fooled into thinking that because God is a forgiving God, sin is no big deal. Sin has consequences. God forgives us, but he doesn't take away all the inevitable trouble that our own bad choices set in motion. Thankfully, though, he loves us enough to be with us even through the difficulties we bring upon ourselves.

Living in Contentment

An important part of moving forward in our lives is learning to be content. Living in contentment doesn't imply that we are stagnant and dull, sticking with the status quo. No, contentment is a quality of the heart that can be found in many of the movers and shakers of our world. It is certainly a quality we want to have as positive women. A content woman is one who accepts the people and the circumstances around her and makes the best of her situation. She has an inner peace, leaving to God those things she cannot change and making a difference where she can. Paul spoke of his own contentment in Philippians 4:11–13: "I have learned to be content whatever the circumstances. I know what it is to be in need, and I know what it is to have plenty. I have learned the secret of being content in any and every situation, whether well fed or hungry, whether living in plenty or in want. I can do everything through him who gives me strength."

Perhaps you have heard or even memorized another common version of that last verse: "I can do all things through Christ who strengthens me" (NKJV). Often Philippians 4:13 is used as a motivational, catchall phrase to imply that we can accomplish anything we set our minds to with God's help. But did you realize that Paul was talking about contentment here? Philippians 4:13 was the key to his contented state.

Can we say the same? Is our contentment found in our relationship with Christ, the one who gives us strength to make it through the various circumstances in our lives? Or do we hang our happiness and contentment on the "if onlys" of life:

- If only I had a better job.

- If only my husband were kind and sensitive.

- If only he worked harder.

- If only I had a bigger house.

- If only my kitchen were updated.

- If only I didn't have this boss.

- If only my childhood hadn't been so bad.

- If only someone would believe in me!

What is the "if only" that is keeping you from being content? Counter that "if only" thinking with a new phrase: "but God can." Pray about your situation, change what ought to be or can be changed, and relinquish everything else to God. Desire contentment as one of the highest virtues.

Paul was undoubtedly one of the greatest "go-getters" in all of Christendom. He was a positive apostle, always encouraging, always teaching, always building new communities of believers. He preached and traveled widely, often finding himself in difficult, even life-threatening circumstances. Yet wherever God led him, he was content in his spirit, and his heart was constantly motivated to press on. Even when he was thrown in prison, he didn't become defeated or discontented. Instead he did what he could do to further the Gospel and encourage the early churches. Many of the letters we have in the New Testament today were written by Paul from a prison cell, including the letter to the Philippians that talks about contentment!

What prison cell are you living in right now? What circumstances are threatening to hold you down and keep you from moving on in your walk with God? Be careful; a discontented spirit will only lead to bitterness, anger, and frustration and will keep you from going forward into the abundant life God has planned for you. What if Paul had sat in his prison cell, feeling sorry for himself and saying, "This is not fair. I shouldn't be here. My ministry is over"? We wouldn't have the benefit of some of the greatest teaching in the Bible! Can you be content and allow God to work through you, too, despite the difficulties you face?

It's Your Choice

As positive women we must make positive choices every day. My hope is that this book has encouraged you to do just that. I pray that you will:

- choose to have faith instead of doubt

- choose to search for wisdom instead of wandering aimlessly in life

- choose to pray instead of worrying and fretting

- choose to experience joy instead of bitterness

- choose to love instead of hate

- choose to live courageously instead of in fear

- choose to have hope instead of despair

- choose to live enthusiastically, knowing that God has a purpose and a plan for your life, and he will empower you to live it out

Press on! Move ahead victoriously on the pathway that God has set before you, despite the inevitable bumps and potholes. Don't waste time complaining about what's wrong, what you don't have, or what other people are doing or thinking. Celebrate what's right in your life. Enjoy what you do have. And most importantly, enjoy being with the people who are dear to you.

As a positive woman, you can be a beacon of light shining in a dark world. You can be a vessel of God's love and joy and forgiveness and hope in a world badly in need of each of these things. Never underestimate the powerful impact you can have on your family, your friends, and the world around you. After all, the power of a positive woman is not your power; it's God's.

Press On!

POWER POINT

⚙ **Read:** Acts 18:2, 18, 24–26; also Romans 16:3–4 and 1 Corinthians 16:19. What part did Priscilla play in the early church? What gifts did she seem to have? Which of the seven principles of a positive woman do you see at work in her life? Do you think her actions had an eternal impact?

💗 **Pray:** Lord, you are a wonderful and loving heavenly Father! You forgive my sins and heal my diseases. You redeem my life from the pit and crown me with love and compassion. You renew my strength like the eagle's. I love you, Lord! Help me to continue moving forward in my walk with you. Tenderly teach me and guide me along the way, and help me to make positive choices each day. Help me to press on for your glory until the day I meet you face to face. In Jesus' name, amen.

💡 **Remember:** "Work hard and cheerfully at whatever you do, as though you were working for the Lord rather than for people" (Colossians 3:23 NLT).

😊 **Do:** Thumb back through this book and highlight or paper clip pages and passages that were particularly meaningful to you. Review the memory verses at the end of each chapter and determine to apply them to your life from this day forward.

Notes

Introduction: The Great Adventure

1. Adapted from Edward Rowell and Bonnie Steffen, *Humor for Preaching and Teaching* (Grand Rapids, Mich.: Baker Books, 1996), 176.

Chapter 1: It's a Girl Thing

1. Adapted from Matthew Henry, *Commentary on the Whole Bible* (Peabody, Mass.: Hendrickson Publishers, Inc., 1991), 6.

2. Edith Deen, *All the Women of the Bible* (Edison, N.J.: Castle Books, 1955), 69.

3. J. C. Webster and K. Davis, ed., *A Celebration of Women* (Southlake, Tex.: Watercolor Books, 2001), 171.

4. Peggy Anderson, *Great Quotes from Great Women* (Lombard, Ill.: Celebrating Excellence Publishing, 1992), 62.

5. Mabel Bartlett and Sophia Baker, *Mothers—Makers of Men* (New York: Exposition Press, 1952), 92.

6. Anderson, *Great Quotes from Great Women,* 11.

7. Gail Rolka, *One Hundred Women Who Shaped World History* (San Meteo, Calif.: Bluewood Books, 1994), 97.

8. Robert Schwaneberg, "Stop the Trains!" *Reader's Digest* (December 2001), 67.

Chapter 2: A Perfect Fit

1. Webster and Davis, *A Celebration of Women,* 146.

2. Kenneth W. Osbeck, *101 Hymn Stories* (Grand Rapids, Mich.: Kregel Publications, 1982), 167.

3. Ibid., 43–44.

4. Frank S. Mead, ed., *12,000 Religious Quotations* (Grand Rapids, Mich.: Baker Book House, 1998), 448.

Chapter 3: The Race of Life

1. Wendy Northcutt, *The Darwin Awards* (New York: Dutton, 2000), 27.

2. Richard J. Foster and Emilie Griffin, ed., *Spiritual Classics* (New York: HarperCollins, 2000), 360.

3. Michael Collopy, *Works of Love Are Works of Peace* (Fort Collins, Colo.: Ignatius Press, 1996), 98.

4. Corrie ten Boom with Jamie Buckingham, *Tramp for the Lord* (Old Tappan, N.J.: Revell Company, 1974), 12.

5. "At Home Live with Chuck and Jenny," *Family Network, Inc.* (Sept. 26, 2001).

Chapter 4: Spiritual Makeover

1. Croft M. Pentz, ed., *The Speaker's Treasury of Four Hundred Quotable Poems* (Grand Rapids, Mich.: Zondervan Publishing House, 1963), 159.

2. Walter Hooper, ed., *God in the Dock* (Grand Rapids, Mich.: Eerdmans, 1970), 55.

3. Jim Cymbala, *Fresh Power* (Grand Rapids, Mich.: Zondervan Publishing, 2001), 200.

4. Mead, *12,000 Religious Quotations,* 134.

5. Ibid., 135.

6. Ibid., 135.

7. John Blanchard, *More Gathered Gold* (Hertfordshire, England: Evangel Press, 1986), 94.

8. Joe Simnacher, *Dallas Morning News,* Thursday, November 29, 2001, A33, 39.

9. Anderson, *Great Quotes by Great Women,* 99.

10. Simnacher, *Dallas Morning News,* A33, 39.

Chapter 5: More Precious Than Rubies

1. Roy B. Zuck, *The Speaker's Quote Book* (Grand Rapids, Mich.: Kregel Publications, 1997), 411.

2. Michael Caputo, *God Seen through the Eyes of the Greatest Minds* (West Monroe, La.: Howard Publishing, 2000), 165.

3. Gorton Carruth and Eugene Ehrlich, *American Quotations* (New York: Gramercy Books, 1988), 599.

4. Angela Beasley, *Minutes from the Great Women's Coffee Club* (Nashville: Walnut Grove Press, 1997), 97.

5. William J. Federer, *America's God and Country* (Coppell, Tex.: Fame Publishing, 1994), 255.

6. Stephen Abbott Northrop, D.D., *A Cloud of Witnesses* (Portland, Oreg.: American Heritage Ministries, 1987), 285.

7. Ibid., 484.

8. Zuck, *The Speaker's Quote Book,* 411.

9. Ibid.

10. *The Pocket Book of Quotations* (New York: Pocket Books, Inc., 1942), 437.

Chapter 6: Winning Wisdom

1. Glenn Van Ekeren, *Speaker's Sourcebook II* (Englewood Cliffs, N.J.: Prentice Hall, 1994), 176–177.

2. Helen Kooiman Hosier, *One Hundred Christian Women Who Changed the Twentieth Century* (Grand Rapids, Mich.: Fleming H. Revell, 2000), 238–241.

3. Ibid.

4. John Bartlett, *Barlett's Familiar Quotations* (Boston: Little, Brown and Company, 1855, 1980), 593.

5. Anderson, *Great Quotes by Great Women,* 99.

Chapter 7: Extra Baggage

1. Blanchard, *More Gathered Gold,* 227.

2. C. S. Lewis, *Letter to Malcolm: Chiefly on Prayer* (New York: Harcourt Brace Javanovich, 1964), 28.

3. C. S. Lewis, *The World's Last Night and Other Essays* (New York: Harcourt Brace Javanovich, 1960), 4–5.

4. Walter B. Knight, *Knight's Master Book of Four Thousand Illustrations* (Grand Rapids, Mich.: Eerdmans Publishing, 1956), 492.

5. Ibid., 485.

Chapter 8: A Simple Guide to Effective Prayer

1. Knight, *Four Thousand Illustrations,* 485.

2. Hank Hanegraaff, *The Prayer of Jesus* (Nashville: Word Publishing, 2001), 10.

3. Rowell and Steffen, *Humor for Preaching and Teaching,* 135.

4. Blanchard, *More Gathered Gold,* 318.

5. Richard J. Foster and James Bryan Smith, *Devotional Classics* (San Francisco: HarperCollins, 1993), 320.

6. Knight, *Four Thousand Illustrations,* 489.

7. *More of God's Words of Life for Women* (Grand Rapids, Mich.: Zondervan Gifts, 2000), 207.

Chapter 9: Experiencing Joy

1. Zuck, *The Speaker's Quote Book,* 215.

2. Used by permission of the author.

3. Edward K. Rowell ed., *Quotes and Idea Starters for Preaching and Teaching* (Grand Rapids, Mich.: Baker Book House, 1996), 92.

4. Knight, *Four Thousand Illustrations,* 347.

Chapter 10: My Life As a Three-Ring Circus

1. *The Secrets of Joy, A Treasury of Wisdom* (Philadelphia: Running Press, 1995), 23.

2. Ibid., 18.

3. Gary Smalley, *Food and Love* (Wheaton, Ill.: Tyndale House Publishers, 2001), 41.

4. John Cook, *The Book of Positive Quotations* (Minneapolis: Fairview Press, 1997), 89.

5. Adapted from Jean Lush, *Women and Stress* (Grand Rapids, Mich.: Fleming H. Revell, 1992), 109–112.

Chapter 11: Friendships in the Fast Lane

1. Alan Loy McGinnis, *The Friendship Factor* (Minneapolis: Augsburg Publishing House, 1979), 25–26.

2. Dale Carnegie, *How to Win Friends and Influence People* (New York: Pocket Books, 1936), 54.

3. Lewis C. Henry, ed., *Five Thousand Quotations for All Occasions* (Garden City, N.Y.: DoubleDay, 1945), 120.

4. Angela B. Freeman, *One Hundred Years of Women's Wisdom* (Nashville: Walnut Grove Press, 1999), 59.

5. Zuck, *The Speaker's Quote Book*, 158.

6. Louise Bachelder, ed., *A Selection on Friendship* (White Plains, N.Y.: Peter Pauper Press, Inc., 1966), 58.

7. *God's Little Devotional Book for Couples* (Tulsa: Honor Books, 1995), 118.

8. Bachelder, *A Selection on Friendship*, 1.

9. Ibid., 25.

Chapter 12: Creative Compassion

1. Knight, *Four Thousand Illustrations*, 395.

2. Anderson, *Great Quotes from Great Women*, 19.

3. Webster and Davis, *A Celebration of Women*, 191.

Chapter 13: High Heels on a Dirt Road

1. K. Golden and B. Findlen, *Remarkable Women of the Twentieth Century* (New York: Friedman Publishing Group, 1998), 20.

2. D. Heyman, "Women of the Year," *US Weekly* (December 10, 2001), 55.

3. Hosier, *One Hundred Christian Women*, 198.

Chapter 14: Facing Fears

1. Blanchard, *More Gathered Gold*, 102.

2. Zuck, *The Speaker's Quote Book*, 151. Adapted from a story by A. L. Kirpatrick.

3. Blanchard, *More Gathered Gold*, 102.

4. Used by permission from Dana Crawford, Dallas, Texas.

Chapter 15: Stop Whining and Start Smiling

1. Gary Thomas, *Christianity Today,* December 3, 1994. Reprinted in *Fresh Illustrations for Preaching and Teaching,* Edward K. Rowell, ed. (Grand Rapids, Mich.: Baker Book House, 1997), 117.

2. Zuck, *The Speaker's Quote Book,* 199.

3. Anderson, *Great Quotes from Great Women,* 11.

4. Cook, *Positive Quotations,* 285.

5. Knight, *Four Thousand Illustrations,* 471.

6. Cook, *Positive Quotations,* 288.

7. *The Secrets of Joy,* 111.

8. Blanchard, *More Gathered Gold,* 156.

Chapter 16: Delicious Morsels

1. Abigail Van Buren, "Dear Abby," *Universal Press Syndicate,* October 13, 2001.

2. Cook, *Positive Quotations,* 271.

3. *The Power of Hope* (New York: Inspirational Press, 1976), 141.

4. Cook, *Positive Quotations,* 272.

Conclusion: Press On!

1. Edward K. Rowell, ed., *Fresh Illustrations for Preaching and Teaching* (Grand Rapids, Mich.: Baker Book House, 1997), 156.

2. Knight, *Four Thousand Illustrations,* 474.

3. Van Ekeren, *Speaker's Sourcebook II,* 279–280.

4. Jennifer McKnight-Trontz, *Yes You Can* (San Francisco: Chronicle Books, 2000), 22.

5. Zuck, *The Speaker's Quote Book,* 131.

6. Ibid.